KING... WITH ... ENS!

Gable and Jean Harlow
Gable and Joan Crawford
Gable and Barbara Stanwyck
Gable and Greta Garbo
Gable and Norma Shearer
Gable and Claudette Colbert
Gable and Myrna Loy
Gable and Vivien Leigh
Gable and Hedy Lamarr
Gable and Greer Garson
Gable and Ava Gardner
Gable and Lana Turner
Gable and Marilyn Monroe
GABLE AND CAROLE LOMBARD

"GABLE ... A LIVELY, GOSSIPY MUST FOR MOVIE BUFFS!"
—*Jackson, Tenn. Sun*

"FABULOUS ... FILLED WITH FASCINATING INCIDENTS."
—*The Arizona Republic*

"IT'S ALL HERE ... FOUR-SQUARE, HONEST AND VERY READABLE!"
—*Publishers Weekly*

Other SIGNET Film Personality Books

☐ **BOGIE: The Biography of Humphrey Bogart by Joe Hyams; with an Introduction by Lauren Bacall.** BOGIE does more than report events. It relives a life. The brawls, the sprees, the razor-edged wisecracks: Hyams describes them all. He recaptures the deep friendships—with Spencer Tracy, Judy Garland, Katharine Hepburn. He probes Bogart's stormy youth; his stubborn climb to stardom; his three rocky marital adventures and his last happy marriage to Lauren Bacall.
(#Y5404—$1.25)

☐ **SPENCER TRACY by Larry Swindell.** In this first biography ever written about the actor, we see Spencer Tracy as he really was—gruff, intensely emotional and completely honest. We see him with his cronies and his long personal and professional relationship with Katharine Hepburn. A complete listing of every film he did and an Index is included. "Meticulous portrait . . . it gives us all the dimensions . . . of a rare, real giant of yesterday's picture parade."—**New York Times Book Review** (#Q4486—95¢)

☐ **CLINT EASTWOOD by Stuart M. Kaminsky.** The candid on-and-off screen story of the world's #1 male superstar. Here is Eastwood the man, one of the most complex and fascinating figures in movieland. Tracing his career from the bit parts in Hollywood to the major movies made by Eastwood's own company, it is the story of the making of a star and legend. Included are 16 pages of great Clint Eastwood photos and a Complete Filmography.
(#W6159—$1.50)

☐ **THE LONG JOURNEY: A BIOGRAPHY OF SIDNEY POITIER by Carolyn Ewers.** You're handsome, talented, wealthy, adored by millions of women—and you're black. You're the Academy Award winning star of **Lilies of the Field, To Sir with Love, Guess Who's Coming to Dinner, For Love of Ivy** and **In the Heat of the Night.** (#P3790—60¢)

GABLE

BY
Chester Williams

SIGNET FILM SERIES

A SIGNET BOOK
NEW AMERICAN LIBRARY
TIMES MIRROR

Library of Congress Catalog Card Number: 68-54388

This is an authorized reprint of a hardcover edition
published by Fleet Press Corporation.

SIGNET TRADEMARK REG. U.S. PAT. OFF. AND FOREIGN COUNTRIES
REGISTERED TRADEMARK—MARCA REGISTRADA
HECHO EN CHICAGO, U.S.A.

SIGNET, SIGNET CLASSICS, MENTOR, PLUME AND MERIDIAN BOOKS
are published by The New American Library, Inc.,
1301 Avenue of the Americas, New York, New York 10019

FIRST PRINTING, JANUARY, 1975

3 4 5 6 7 8 9

PRINTED IN THE UNITED STATES OF AMERICA

Contents

☆
GABLE

CHAPTER 1

The Early Years

Clark Gable died eight years ago. Eight light years ago.

Today, chic Japanese stores in New York City peddle Clark Gable glassware and Clark Gable scarves. At discotheques across the land, teenagers undulate to the big beat in shimmering eeriness as huge Clark Gable slides flash across their flesh and onto barren walls. Frenetic girls there wear Clark Gable paper dresses. The strange beds they may share, hours later, might well be stationed under large Clark Gable "hang-up" posters.

Elsewhere, a teenybopper sits before his home television screen watching a late movie, starring vintage Gable. The youth's parents also are in the room, quiet, holding hands and feeling nostalgic over a romantic era when manliness was embodied in the box-office hero with the neatly trimmed mustache. Their son's smirk is hidden behind a frozen face.

The cool generation also mocks Clark Gable at film festivals, revivals of his greatest starring roles, off California campuses and near other colleges in many states.

Yet the first sixty years of this century spanned an era. They were the Clark Gable years. Today's silver screen belches nudity, sadism, pseduo-intellectualism, psychedelic claptrap and a frivolous blur of the sexes. We see overt displays of masturbation, homosexuality, and perversion. It is part of the kicky, "free" era of the profane word and the profane promotion of film. These are times when the straight-forward approach to sex and action, hallmarks of Clark Gable appearances before the magic lanterns of Hollywood, are passé.

If this era that followed Gable is different, so too was the one that preceded the stocky performer. Clark Gable drew his first breath on February 1, 1901, in Cadiz, Ohio, as a blizzard raged outside. Halfway across the world, England was burying Queen Victoria, and interring with her the end of formal prudism. Gable, then, became truly a man for his time—he spanned the orderly hypocrisy of Victorian life and a flickering world deflected from reality by narcotics, protest, and the blare of mass media.

To scan the mountain of pap already prepared on Gable and to speak with those who say they knew him is to wade through a morass of legend which grows with the passage of time. At his death, news magazines faithfully reported his weight at birth as twelve pounds; early biographers set his first weight at anywhere from nine and a half pounds to eleven. One might suppose that cinema historians of yet another era, after nutritional marvels yet undiscovered expand the size and longevity of the human race, may write of an infant Gable forcing his first scream from a heftier-than-twelve-pound body. Such minutia are unimportant.

We do know that Adelia Gable's only child—William Clark—was falsely registered as "F" (for female), a clerical error that caused his father not a little discomfort until it was corrected with the slash of a red pencil.

The father, William H., was a Pennsylvania Dutchman who Anglicized his name, Goebel, before marrying Adelia Hershelman, daughter of Dutch-born farm folk who settled in Meadville, Pennsylvania. Papa Bill Gable's life was divided between farming and wildcatting in oil fields. In fact, it was an oil strike in Harrison County, Ohio, that brought the Gables from Meadville to Cadiz, for the opportunities of living near and working at the Bricker oil fields.

In Billy's (as Clark was known through childhood) infancy, his father roamed wherever oil strikes beckoned, while Clark was reared by grandparents on both sides. Adelia Gable never recovered her health after the birth of her son.

In fact, Adelia's sickliness gave way to another piece of the Gable legend, a bit of falsity perpetuated by Hollywood press agents and fostered by one of his more celebrated wives of later years, Carole Lombard.

There was some anxiety, the story goes, on the part of Dr. John S. Campbell, who examined Adelia during her pregnancy; he told her she might not survive the childbirth. She confided this fear to her sister, and is said to have written eighteen letters to her unborn, numbered them in order, and mandated that Josie read each one every six months to Clark until such time as he could read them himself. The letters, the legend says, were to be Adelia's voice from the grave, to enable her offspring to "grow up knowing the sort of person his mother was, and the sort of person I would like him to be," in the words of one Hollywood press release. More likely, it was the sort of nonsense that came from the typewriters of creative press agents, intent on moving the starstruck to the box office through the sort of sentimentalism rampant on early movie screens.

Adelia died when Clark was ten months old and was buried in a nearby Catholic cemetery. Aunt Josie and another Hershelman, her brother Tom, took turns helping rear father Gable's bulky baby, but Bill Gable worried lest his son grow up in the Catholic faith of his mother. (Clark was baptized at birth.)

In less than two years, Clark Gable had a stepmother, Jennie Dunlap, a kind, plain Methodist from a mining town near Cadiz who had seemed destined for a life of spinsterhood until the senior Gable met her one day near the haberdashery where she worked. The remarriage also brought to a head the issue of Clark Gable's Catholicism. Uncle Tom insisted that Adelia had asked, on her deathbed, that the boy be reared in her faith. "If she did, she kept it from me," argued Bill Gable. He allowed young Clark to spend an occasional Christmas and parts of the summer with the Hershelmans, but only in exchange for the promise that they "not try to turn him into a Catholic."

Good times came to the Gables, who lived cozily in a two-story, three-bedroom, well-furnished home that prompted one neighbor to describe them as "not rich . . . but they had all they needed." One family possession was a Model T Ford coupe, which propelled father Gable to weekday work away from home and to weekends at the family hearth. Jennie and Clark developed a close, happy relationship. She was a good cook, played the piano and sang, and gave her stepson a splendid birthday party in each of his early years. "She spoiled me and I loved it," Clark said of their relationship later

"I recall having the first bicycle of any kid in town."

Those who grew up with Clark also recall his "large gray eyes, long dark lashes and rosy cheeks." A woman who had been ahead of him in school said she remembered "seeing him playing in the street when he was too young to go to school. He was a sunny little fellow, happy and responsive, riding up and down the street on a stick horse, with a red sweater, toboggan cap and leggings. He was full of fun." Another, closer friend, remembers "Billy" as having "the loudest voice of any boy in the neighborhood."

The Gable voice was on full display at the family piano, but Jennie's attempts to teach him that instrument failed. A player piano at the neighboring Means Hotel spanked out the jerky tunes of the era, and Billy Gable first learned to dance to its music, although clumsily. He grew quickly, was always the tallest in his class, and developed the shyness that often accompanies early ungainliness.

Years later, one of his first dates—prompted by a Hollywood feature writer—looked back to their "relationship" and sputtered: "Kissing games? The only times I became angry at Billy was over a kissing game. Whenever we played 'post office' he always insisted on being postmaster because then he didn't have to kiss me or anybody else." (We can presume that one to be true since it does not perpetuate his image as a great lover.) But we might also conjecture that Gable lost his virginity on a haystack in Hopedale, where sex experiments traditionally satisfied the curiosity of the sons and daughters of Ohio farm folk in the years preceding the wider distribution of automobiles.

Billy passed his time in the mundane diversions of

rural America. He attended frequent church functions, fished in neighboring streams, and played the alto horn in a local band that performed at weddings and picnics. His physique was developing along lines fated to become familiar to millions of movie-goers, from hauling hundred-pound sacks of flour from a horse-drawn cart to general stores. Young Billy also took odd jobs carrying water for coal miners.

But schoolwork had little appeal for the young Buckeye. Except for good grades in spelling, he showed little aptitude. Legend has him yearning to become a doctor in those years, but there is no evidence to support it.

Hopedale High had its social moments, too, even for the shy, gangling Billy Gable. One of his friends, Tommy Lewis, had a sister named Thelma, a redhead and "the prettiest girl in town," according to those with memories fuzzed and eager to share in the glories of having a movie star come from their community. Young Gable and Thelma became an item at Epworth League meetings and at Sunday school picnics. "Clark was my first date," Thelma later told biographer Jean Garceau. "He was not particularly good-looking. His ears were too large."

His high school years also marked Clark Gable's first appearance on a stage, as a rough-and-tumble type in *The Arrival of Kitty*. Thelma had the title role, and Clark Gable's name appeared far down in the handwritten credits. Gable made more of a name for himself as a slugging second baseman and basketball player on Hopedale varsities.

A more orderly life once again beckoned Clark's father, who sold both his Hopedale home and his oil-rigging gear to invest in a larger farm and house in Ravenna, Ohio. Gable recalled his new environment with less than affection: "Working on that farm meant getting up at four in the morning every day in the year, spring, summer, fall and winter, and the winters sure are cold in Ohio. I fed the hogs, the rest of the stock, plowed in the morning until every muscle ached, and forked hay in the hot sun until I was sweating crops of calluses. I did what I was expected to do on that farm, but I just didn't have what it takes."

And if one thing griped him more than any other, it was "to ride on that bus every day with a lot of kids half my age." That November, in 1917, Clark Gable announced to his dad that he was home from school for good. Although Gable was to become an avid reader and self-educated in adulthood, his formal schooling ended right then and there.

Memories of Hopedale lured him back to the scene of his triumphs on a high school athletic field. He commuted the sixty miles often, returning to his chums to strum a ukelele and join in choruses of "For Me and My Gal" and "Where the Blackeyed Susans Grow." A month later, Billy asked his father if he could again spend more time in Hopedale, hauling water for its miners; they were "paying five dollars a day for that now," he said ecstatically.

One week after his son renewed such work at the mines, Gable senior opened a letter from Billy and read that he wanted to purchase the old family Model T, for $175. "Sure," said his father. But wheels for a youngster in 1917 meant the same as they do today: freedom and grandiose ideas.

Gable conspired with Andy Means, a Hopedale buddy, to seek adventure in a big city. Akron was experiencing boom times as the nation's wartime economy and a burgeoning rubber industry there beckoned farm youths from neighboring Indiana, Pennsylvania, and a host of Southern states, as well as from the farms and hamlets of central Ohio.

Lively arguments followed in the Gable household. "Haven't you got a good enough home here?" his father implored. But Jennie Gable understood, and Andy's arrival from Hopedale meant that the two lads were off to catch an early train for "the rubber capital of the world."

They arrived in Akron juggling straw suitcases and food parcels that Jennie had packed, to solve the mysteries of women working dark streets, of dancing into the early hours, and of swigging hard liquor and working in ear-shattering rubber plants.

Firestone Steel Products hired Clark Gable as a clerk at the munificent rate of $95 a month. Andy signed on with the same company, molding treads on tires; they rented rooms in adjoining houses.

Those first footloose years though, were not what one might imagine for a young man destined to become the male sex symbol of his generation: "I never had any full-fledged romances in my youth because I never had time for them," he told an interviewer. "I was always trying to stay one step ahead of the breadlines in the early days. You can't be romantically inclined when all of your effort is being put into getting a job or holding one." It was an era preceding the eight-hour day, five-day work week. The hours were long, and Sundays off meant resting up for the rigors of the next six days ahead.

When a postwar depression struck Akron, thousands

were laid off—including Andy Means and Billy Clark Gable. Means returned to Hopedale, but Gable stayed on as a salesman in a clothing store. Even that didn't work out, however, as hard times forced a layoff of clerical help at Gates and Kittle's dry-goods establishment.

Gable had to find a new direction and, contrary to earlier editions of *Who's Who in America*, it was not discovered at the University of Akron. (That bit of folklore was given added credence by press agents in later years, who placed Gable in medical school.) The truth is almost as interesting and more in the tradition of movie-magazine writing: a production of *The Bird of Paradise* lured Gable to Akron Music Hall for his first evening in a theater. He returned to the music hall often, to drift around the stage door and attempt to mingle with the performers. Gable, unmistakably, was stage-struck.

One night he gathered enough courage to talk to two actors, who invited him to watch the next performance from the wings. One thing led to another and leading man Ed Clark Lilley agreed to give Clark Gable a "job" as callboy. "I can't pay you anything," he told him, "but if you want to learn this business, being a callboy isn't too bad a way to start."

Gable slept in the theater, showered at a nearby YMCA, managed meals from the tips received running errands for the cast, and eventually spoke his first lines on a legitimate stage, as a walk-on: "Good evening, sir."

But tragedy once again loomed in the Gable family. Stepmother Jennie became incurably ill, and young Clark interrupted his difficult days as a theater apprentice to return to Ravenna. He was at Jennie's bedside when she died.

Soon, the old arguments echoed through the house. His father wanted Clark to give up his "shenanigans" and go with him to Oklahoma, where new oil booms once again promised prosperity. "I won't give up the theater," shouted his headstrong son. He was more ambitious than ever; he decided to try his luck in New York.

Once more, the best he could manage in a depression-ridden city was a job as a callboy, but this time it was on Broadway, in the company of some of the greatest names of the stage.

Gable found himself knocking on the doors of John and Lionel Barrymore, to remind them: "Half an hour, sir," as curtain time neared. They were in the midst of a 179-performance run of *The Jest*, which opened on September 19, 1919. Gable struggled through poverty conditions, living in a small walkup apartment and taking sparse snacks at lunch stands. When *The Jest* closed, so did Gable's chances for survival. An unending search for work in a company—any company—proved unfruitful. Clark decided that his only choice was a return to life with father, near Bigheart, Oklahoma, where the rigors of working as an oil-field apprentice was to bring him $12 a day.

Once again, the young Gable frame began taking on new muscle as Clark chopped wood to fuel boiler fires, as he worked a heavy sledgehammer, pounding edges on fiery drill bits held firm by a blacksmith. He would lug heavy pieces of pipe into place as they were coupled for penetration into the oil-rich soil. It was a hellish life of sharing beds with whores, of watching crooked gamblers bilk gullible oilmen, of bootleg gin, drunken brawls, and frequent knifings. Yet Gable never lost faith in a future on the stage. What little he earned, he managed to put some of it into savings against the day when opportunity again beckoned. About $300 left to him by grandfather Hershelman, who died, also went into the kitty.

About a year later, news of a Kansas City repertory company sent Clark packing. "I told the stubborn mule that if he left me this time, he needn't come back," said his father. They were not to communicate again for years.

At this juncture of Gable's life, the imagery of press agents who were to follow again appears to cloud his true biography. Myriad accounts report of his times with the "Jewell Stock Players" (an actual company with that name was appearing farther north and west in the early twenties but never performed in Kansas City), of a captivating leading lady, age forty-five, who had lost an eye in an on-stage duel and who taught young Gable more in her dressing room than she did on-stage.

Gable's recollections of his two years with the Kansas City tent company make for less interesting reading: "They gave me a break young actors do not get anymore. I was paid only ten dollars a week. Even so, I think they gave me the job only because they needed someone with a strong back to do the heavy work." Gable spent more time with physical chores off-stage than acting on—keeping horses, driving stakes, serving as a callboy. He even took up the cornet to help lure theatergoers into the tent. "That was the most godawful thing," he once complained to columnist Dorothy Kilgallen. "We used to climb into old clown suits and stand on the corner playing 'Marching Through Georgia' to get them in."

When the driving winter of 1922 prevented audiences from leaving their homes, the tent company found itself impoverished in Butte, Montana. Gable was down to his last few dollars. He boarded a refrigerator train headed for Portland and, shivering all the way, rode rails moving toward the warmth of the West Coast. "It was either that or go to work in the copper mines," he said.

As the train slowed down for a stop in Bend, Oregon, a tired and hungry Gable got off near the Brooks Hanlon Lumber Company. "I went inside to get warm and found that they were hiring men, no questions asked. In ten minutes, I was on the payroll." For the next three months, he pulled a long cross-saw against the push of a huge Swede named Thorsen. Gable's hands became chapped and raw. He would heal them with biting vinegar, and would soften that ointment's sting with applications of lard. As before, Gable practiced frugality and left with enough money saved to try his luck in yet another metropolis—Portland. "It was the nearest big city, and I thought I might find a theater there," he reasoned.

With a new suit on his back and his indefatigable spirit intact, Clark Gable found himself behind the tie counter at Meier and Frank's Department Store, beside a twenty-three-year-old co-worker, Earl Larimore. Besides a temporary stint as tie salesmen, they shared a love for the theater. And Larimore, who had acted in productions at Oregon State and whose family had performed professionally for generations, had connections. Larimore was moonlighting as actor and director of the Red Lantern Players, then featuring *Nothing But the*

Truth. His new-found friend Gable watched performances every night from backstage.

Their theater talk behind the tie counter was interrupted one day when Kirk McKean, owner of the Astoria Players, which performed a hundred miles northwest of Portland, asked Larimore to join the company as actor and part-time director. Gable asked his friend if he could tag along to try his luck. Soon after the company opened, on July 23, 1922, Clark Gable played in blackface for the first and only time in his career, as Eliza, a cook who closes the third act as chief of police. (In *The Villain Still Pursued Her,* another Players production, Gable was wheeled on-stage in a baby carriage.)

But the Astoria company was to play a more significant role in Clark—or Billy, as he still was known—Gable's life. He was to fall in love with one of the finest ladies he would know in a life that carried him through five marriages and a score of affairs.

Frances Doerfler (soon to change her first name to "Franz," presumably better to squeeze it into a marquee) was reading for an ingenue role with the Astoria Players when she noticed the rugged young Gable offering root beer to a Portland society girl competing for the part. Minutes later, after the socialite was sent home and Franz won the role, Clark made her the same offer, and Frances snubbed him. She also rebuffed his offer to walk her home.

Franz was two years older than Gable—his gravitation to older women was consistent through the first half of his life—and she was beautiful. He walked her home, anyway, and overlooked her icy indifference. He became petulant, possessive, terribly overattentive. Days later, he told Franz he was completely smitten with her.

Meanwhile, her success with the Astoria group was not matched by her paramour. "If he [Gable] had experience at all with any such traveling show," said the wife of Astoria's producer, "it must have been restricted to putting up and taking down the tent. He could not have been on the stage even a few weeks without learning more than he knew in that summer of 1922. He could get on and off the stage, but did not even always manage that successfully."

But the budding Gable-Doerfler romance was to perpetuate his career with the Astoria Players. "In the end we took him along," explained producer Rex Jewell, "but only because it seemed to mean so much to Franz Doerfler. By that time she and Billy Gable were in love. Naturally, she wanted him to be with her. But this was nothing compared to his desire to be with her. I have rarely, in fact, seen more of a lovesick puppy."

Astoria, Oregon, became the scene of rough-and-tumble theater. Populated by fifteen thousand, mostly rugged Finns, Astoria seemed a good market for diversions of any kind for her hard-working lumberjacks and fishermen. On opening night of the season, the house was packed for a farce, *It Can't Be Done,* (a plagiarism of another play, *Nothing But the Truth.* The management sought to escape from paying royalties).

Halfway through the first act, the lights went out. In the darkness, boos and hisses gave way to the smashing of chairs in the orchestra. Owner McKean, candle in hand, ventured to center stage to divert the audience with impressions of Harry Lauder, until an oil lamp could be found.

But before full lighting was restored, a woman in the back rows complained loudly that she was being raped; when the house lights went up, she was seen fully clothed and not the least bit embarrassed by her claim. By final curtain, the audience was charmed by the performance on-stage, and the cast spent several happy and relieved moments taking curtain calls.

As it turned out, the blackout was caused by an unsympathetic Astoria Light and Power Company, impatient for payment of its monthly bill. And the man responsible for making the payment had legged it across the Canadian border with the electric money and much of the receipts from the sellouts of the first week.

There were added financial difficulties along the way, including the shutting off of credit for the troupe in nearby hash houses. Several of the better performers left the company for other opportunities, where regular meals were less of a problem. For William Gable (as he was carried on the playbills) it spelled opportunity. He was given larger roles by default: a village doctor in *Corrine of the Circus,* a character actor in *Blundering Billy.* It was heady stuff, and he didn't mind at all that his share of the company's profits ranged from $1.30 to $10 a week. But his were hardly stellar performances. "He hasn't fallen down since that first night," said Jewell of Gable's acting. "Now he only stammers, staggers and stumbles all over the stage."

Gable's romance with Franz was flourishing, however, and Miss Doerfler was suffering less than her fellow troupers from the food shortage; she had moved into an aunt's home (from where she also smuggled sandwiches to her paramour to keep up his strength for a budding stage career.) Her parents were soon to open a letter informing them of Franz's engagement to "a William C. Gable."

More troubles beset the Astoria group, including the loss of its theater in a fire that swept downtown Astoria. The company folded, and Franz brought Clark to the Doerfler Silverton Farm in Willamette Valley. There, he took odd jobs, including work with the Silverton Lumber Company, at little more than $3 a day. He again began saving from the little he earned, and when he amassed $100 he asked Franz to marry him. She told her twenty-one-year-old fiancé that their future looked too uncertain. Gable, heartbroken, couldn't bear to stay on, and Franz Doerfler was to carry a torch for her Clark for the rest of her life. Although uncommonly attractive, charming and desirable, she was to spurn a score of marriage proposals through the years and never married.

CHAPTER 2

Enter Josephine Dillon

Legend has it that a distressed Clark Gable rebounded from his rebuff from Franz Doerfler with some distracting work as a lineman with a Portland telephone company. "One of the last phones he fixed," according to *Time* Magazine, "was at the theater of the Red Lantern Players, where Josephine Dillon, then in her late thirties, was the resident stage director. She taught him diction, projection and carriage, and married him when he was twenty-three."

It was merely one more version of the neat story Hollywood circulated for years: Franz Doerfler left Gable . . . Gable pouted . . . he met Josephine Dillon on the rebound . . . they married and she helped prepare him for stardom.

But life, as the many who have had their complications know, does not divide into such concise episodes. There was more than one reconciliation between Gable and Franz, months—and even years—after their breakup. Franz had taken a job with a Portland stock company, and Gable did, indeed, work in Portland—first as a clerk for an automobile-accessory company and then selling classified ads for the Portland *Oregonian,* for $15 a week. One ad he placed called for telephone linemen (and a chance to get outdoors). He answered the ad himself, and got the job.

Ironically, it was Franz who steered Gable to Josephine Dillon; she had heard of the drama coach and recommended that Clark see her. But Miss Dillon never had her phone repaired by Clark Gable. And divergent schedules for Franz and Gable deepened their separation.

While Josephine Dillon was drawing her first impressions of her new pupil, ("He was a young man, deep, quiet and thoughtful . . . a gloomy, deadpan Dutchman with three hundred years of Pennsylvania Dutch behind him.") the strained Gable-Doerfler relationship worsened. Gable at one point told Franz he "no longer loved her," that all he cared about were his studies with Miss Dillon. Two weeks later he called to say he "must have been crazy" and that if she still wanted him, they would marry "at any time, and the sooner the better." But time kept slipping away. And the gentle, soft-speaking drama coach was more and more becoming a part of Gable's life.

Miss Dillon and her pupil were reading parts together in *Hamlet, Romeo and Juliet,* and from the newest Eugene O'Neill scenarios. Gable progressed to a point where she thought him ready for his first role: as Menian Deacon, in *Miss Lulu Bett.* At the same time, they were drawing closer to each other. A preview of the developing triangle was on display one afternoon when Josephine and Clark dropped by at the Portland theater, where Franz was featured, to borrow some scenery.

It was the first time that these first women in his

young life had met. "She upstaged me that evening," recalled Franz of Clark's tutor. "What was more important was that my love did, too. That was one lesson, upstaging people, he had learned from her which he had not described to me."

Things between Clark and Franz cooled to such a point where Miss Dillon could place W. C. Gable (as he was to be billed on the program) into the same company with Franz. There was to be no reconciliation. And when Josephine Dillon closed her own troupe to move to Hollywood, to open a new school, Gable soon left for the film capital as well.

It was 1924, and he was one of the few performers venturing west for a stage career. Let the others look to duplicate the film success stories of Charlie Chaplin, Douglas Fairbanks, and Harold Lloyd, he thought. "I'm still interested only in the legitimate stage."

Earlier biographers would have us believe that Gable, down to his last dollar, "ran into" Josephine Dillon "on a Hollywood street," and that she then invited him to stay at her $20-a-month bungalow while she moved in with a friend—presumably to preserve propriety.

It seems more likely that the Gable-Dillon relationship moved past the friendly-buss-on-the-cheek stage months earlier, back in Oregon. A vibrant male and a lively woman, such as they were, who worked as closely and intensely as they did, were not likely candidates for long-term status as platonic friends. Moreover, there would have been no reason for Gable not to call her up when he arrived in Hollywood from an all-night train ride. There was less reason for her to move from her own flat just because the handsome young actor moved in. They were married six months later, on December 13, 1924.

The first Mrs. Gable was born in Denver in 1888, was educated at Stanford and in Italy, and came from distinguished California stock. Her father was a renowned judge and prosecutor, yet the Dillon household seemed always filled with lively talk about the arts. One Dillon daughter became an opera singer who debuted in Italy and Josephine's other sister gained wide recognition as a fine composer. Josephine worked her way through theatrical ranks to a starring role on Broadway, and later became a lecturer and a leading participant in the Army's Liberty Theater program during the First World War. Most of all, though, she enjoyed teaching actors their trade which came to include no less than Gary Cooper, Lupe Velez (and Clark Gable, of course) in her roster of Dillon-taught cinema stars.

The marriage, to a woman thirteen years older than Gable, continued his pattern of being attracted to older women. This facet of Gable's psyche has been much analyzed over the years. The loss of a mother before he was old enough to know her, and of a revered stepmother while he was still a child were factors. So, too, was his early ungainliness, which led to boyish withdrawl from his young society. As his rugged handsomeness developed rapidly, a mature confidence in himself was slower to develop. He seemed to need the comfort of maturity in his women during this stage in his life.

The newlyweds settled in Josephine's bungalow; Clark bought a used car for under $60 and diligently set off each day in search of interviews with theatrical producers. His bride took a job reading while waiting for her drama school roster to fill.

Gable fared no better with the legitimate productions in southern California than he had in Akron, Kansas City, and Portland. He turned to movies, and found a bit part in *White Man*, ten days' employment that brought him $150 and a temporary appetite for a film career. But work was scarce and extras were plentiful; the best he could find was an occasional stint in a crowd scene at $5 a day. His scale moved up to $7.50 when he worked in *The Merry Widow*, starring John Gilbert and Mae Murray, but the going was hard indeed. (Years later, after he became a great star, Gable was known to be exceptionally considerate of movie extras. It was said that his early, difficult years at that task were never forgotten.)

In the meantime, Josephine worked her young husband unmercifully. She made him spend hours of tedium at breathing exercises, to deepen a voice that was much too squeaky for the emerging sound films. She made him walk up and down stairs endlessly, to change his lumbering gait into a more graceful walk. Although their budget was tight, she would pack him off to the movies several times a week, to study the performances of those she felt he should emulate. And Josephine started him on a path of self-education; she force-fed his reading of the biographies of great men and of the works of Dickens, Zola, and Thackeray. Then, too, there were the Hollywood parties, for more work and little play. There, Josephine would quietly tutor her husband in the polite ways of society. Gable's growing polish and confidence were her reward.

In fact, when another opportunity came, he reacted better then ever before. He took a $35-a-week walk-on role in a midsummer, 1925 production of *Romeo and*

Juliet, on its West Coast leg of a nationwide tour. He became the production's "leader of the extras," and was very popular with his fellow performers. Stage roles in "*What Price Glory, Madame X,* and *Lady Frederick* followed.

But Gable's progress under company directors rubbed his tutor-wife the wrong way. Josephine would come to rehearsals and openly criticize the way her husband was being managed—much to Clark's embarrassment and the annoyance of the rest of the cast. Before long, she was barred from the theater.

It was during this tenure that Billy Gable became Clark Gable. Hollywood, as might be expected, has a legend for the event. It seems that Gable and Josephine were shopping on Hollywood Boulevard when they stopped in Clark's Dollar Shirt Shop for a purchase. "That's a great shirt," Gable is reported to have said. But Josephine's mind, as always, was on his career. Looking back at the shop's window, she mused: "Don't you think Clark might be a good stage name for you to use, dear? After all, it is your middle name." Whether or not this romanticized version is true, the fact is the star-to-be's days as Billy Gable were finished at this point in his career.

But the new name brought nothing but the same old bad luck. Gable began to suffer from indigestion. He also took to fetishes in his culinary habits; for days on end he would eat nothing but one kind of food and its derivatives. There were days of eating only tomatoes, tomato soup, tomato salad, and tomato juice. Then he would switch to oranges, then apples, then back to tomatoes or another fruit or vegetable.

The following summer, a revival of *The Copperhead*

brought the great Lionel Barrymore back to a Hollywood stage for its starring role. When Clark Gable approached him for a job with the company, Barrymore remembered him as the young man who served as his callboy years before in New York. Gable was given a juvenile role.

Perhaps it was the excitement of working with his boyhood idol that was to blame, or that the overdose of instruction from his wife rattled him, but on opening night of *The Copperhead*, Gable stumbled near a stage prop and lost his hat. The hat fell into the prop—a deep well—and the crowd roared as the young actor reached easily down to pluck it out.

With the embarrassing laughter still ringing in his ears, Gable moved off-stage to catch a sharp barrage from Barrymore. The more Barrymore raged about his "stupidity," the more Gable became convinced that this night was his last with that company. But Barrymore's liking for the lad is said to have saved him for the rest of the run.

One friend in the cast described his carriage with these words: "Persons who knew Clark Gable only after he made his sensational success in Hollywood cannot imagine how clumsy and callow he was in those days. You admired him for the reasons you would later on—his great warmth, his fascination for everything and, oddly enough, for his innocence. But physically, he was as clumsy as an ox."

As Gable's career struggled along, so, too, did his marriage. Arguments became more frequent, as did his slamming of doors and irate stalking out of the house in anger. Often, he would not return until the following morning. At first, it was mostly to brood over an early-hour poker game. But then he sought the comforts of other women. And more often than not, they were older women.

One was Jane Cowl, sixteen years his senior, who had turned a stunning performance of Juliet just the summer before, despite her years, Jane had gone through a marriage with a *New York Times* drama critic before meeting Gable in the southern California Shakespeare production. She first noticed Gable in a line-up of prospective spear-carriers, and promptly asked director Lillian Albertson to hire him. "I want him," Jane told Lillian and, after a dramatic pause, added: "For the play, of course." That week, Gable had the role—and was dining nightly with Miss Cowl privately, in her room.

Then Franz Doerfler reappeared in Gable's life—briefly and for the next-to-last time—when he left for San Francisco with a MacLoon-Albertson production of *The Lullaby*. He was performing at the Curran Theater, across the street from where Franz was working as a dance instructor. They met each other accidentally, had several pleasant dates, but Gable seemed to have other prospects in mind. He had signed on with Pauline Frederick's company of *Madame X*, and the almost-forty beauty was in the habit of having her back rubbed nightly by handsome young actors. Gable won that role as well as a small part in her play.

This fling with Pauline was one of a string of romances during Gable's first marriage. Pauline, considered to be one of the great *femmes fatales* of her era, had bankrupted one husband and ranked high in the scandal stories after a young actor was found dead. At his side was a suicide note blaming his unrequited love for Pauline. The Frederick name also was filed in divorce actions of several Hollywood wives.

It was an era for the screaming headline, for gossip items from Hollywood, when directors would stimulate romance in love scenes with a chorus of off-camera violins. Often, when Pauline Frederick brought Gable to her quarters, two gypsy types bowed furiously on their violins through the evening. Gable would return from these evenings complaining of an overdose of oysters Pauline had thrust upon him (she considered them an exquisite aphrodisiac), and of a woman "who acts every night as though she never expected to see another man." By this time Gable had moved from his bungalow home with Josephine to a bachelor's flat.

His next role, in *Chicago*, with Nancy Carroll, brought a Gable portrayal of Jake the reporter. Some believe he originated the hat-to-the-back-of-the-head style for cocky reporters that soon became an accepted stereotype, in city rooms as well as in movies and on the stage.

Nancy Carroll turned her role of Roxy into a vehicle for a $5,000-weekly contract with Paramount studios. But Gable, who was offered a screen test at the time, turned it down. "Why waste my time and your money?" he asked a talent scout. "I've tried movie work often enough to become convinced I have nothing Hollywood wants." He signed a contract with a Houston stock company instead.

The trek to Texas brought a deeper separation from his wife, who remained steadfast in fostering his career even after their life together was virtually over. Josephine encouraged him to take the Houston assignment for the experience it offered (he was contracted to play the second lead in the company). The fact that he had earned only $1,000 over the prior two years also was a factor. He welcomed a chance for a steady income.

Yet Josephine couldn't bear the separation from her prodigy and joined him with the Gene Lewis Players, an active group that presented Texans with two different plays each week. Within twelve weeks Gable was moved up to lead roles and a $200-weekly salary. His first break came with the role of Matt Burke in Eugene O'Neill's *Anna Christie*. But Josephine's penchant for coaching her Clark again was too much for the company's producer and director. She was asked to leave, and returned to California.

Meanwhile, her estranged husband was becoming quite the idol of the ladies in his audiences. One seductive theater-goer, taken by his bedroom eyes, sent him a wardrobe of clothes from her father's store. Another offered him half of the insurance business she inherited if he would divorce Josephine and marry her.

With the close of the Gene Lewis Players' tour, several of its performers veterans of minor roles on Broadway, invited Clark to accompany them to New York to try their luck together. "I couldn't get New York out of my mind," Gable said. "When I went there this time, I'd have letters of recommendation from the Houston Company. It was too good a chance to miss. I settled for New York."

It was the fall of 1928. New York City was moving through another year of unprecedented prosperity. Shoeshine boys and common laborers were playing the stock market—and winning—as the market kept moving upward. There was an air of revelry, a fine mood for diversions such as the theater. Gable soon found himself signing a contract to play opposite Zita Johann, the female lead in *Machinal*.

Four weeks of rehearsal preceded a three-day preview run in New Haven. "I was the typical stock company actor from the provinces," Gable later said of the experience, "and I panicked at the thought of Broadway. I guess I just tried too hard." On opening night in New Haven, he muttered his lines and floundered about on the stage. Next morning, at rehearsal, he was convinced he would be replaced. But producer Arthur Hopkins avoided Gable's anxious glances and the actor prepared for another performance.

The pressure mounted, and Gable's next two evenings before audiences were worse than his first. He had totally lost his confidence. While the rest of the cast was packing for the train trip to New York, Gable gathered his courage and approached Hopkins asking to resign.

Hopkins would have none of it. He remembered Gable's fine performances through earlier rehearsals. "Just relax," he said simply. Days later, on September 7, 1928, Gable was to appear on opening night, in Broadway's Plymouth Theater. The house was packed. Hopkins came to his dressing room, and as the callboy came by to remind Gable there were ten minutes to curtain, the producer suggested that he forget about the filled house. "Just play it the way you rehearsed it," he said, in a low, encouraging voice. Gable did.

Late that evening, Gable grabbed the first editions from a Broadway newsstand. *The Times* found him to be "an engaging adventurer" who "played the casual, good-humored lover without a hackneyed gesture." The *Tele*graph told its readers that Gable was "young, vigorous and brutally masculine." *The New Yorker* later termed him "excellent as the lover."

Despite generally good reviews, however, the play was to run just twelve weeks. Gable then became one more unemployed actor among many making regular calls along Broadway in search of a part.

As the first snows of winter fell on the metropolis, Josephine Dillon Gable journeyed across the nation to urge him to return with her to Hollywood for a film career. "We had drifted apart," he said of their marriage, and he still had nothing but disdain for the movie colony. He stayed in New York as she went home. That March, she filed for a divorce. "What the hell do I care," bellowed Gable. "I never intend to marry again. If she wants a divorce, let her have it."

Machinal, as it turned out, meant a good deal more to Gable than his first important role on Broadway. In the audience on that opening night was a stunning Houston divorcée, Maria (Ria) Langham, her teenaged daughter George Anna, and a son from still another marriage, Booth Franklin. Ria's brother was an actor, and they came to the Plymouth Theater to see several performers whom they had known on the Houston stage. "We went backstage to visit after the performance," she said. "I had seen Clark in stock in Houston but had never met him. After the show, we were introduced, and he went on to supper with us."

The thrice-divorced aristocrat, seventeen years older than Gable, was small, regal and extremely attractive, with soft auburn hair, bobbed in the fashion of the late twenties. In time, she was to become the second Mrs. Gable.

CHAPTER 3

Ria Langham, The Thirties, and Stardom

Ria Langham, who was first married before Clark Gable was in school, spurred his off-camera development. She was tasteful, intelligent, cultivated, and chic. Her dinner parties were impeccable, with gourmet-quality cuisine served elegantly; her home was a model of gracious decor. She spoke well, looked good, and dressed in the best of taste. And she did all she could to make Gable a perfect-gentleman counterpart to her ladylike bearing.

His new tutor—in the ways of the aristocracy—had learned about the cultivated life from others. Born Maria Franklin, in Kentucky, she moved with her family to Macomb, Illinois, at an early age and there became the teenaged bride of William Prentiss. She bore him one son. Months later, Ria left Prentiss for a divorcée's gay life in Houston. To make ends meet, she took a sales job at J. J. Sweeney's, a jewelry shop with a first-class clientele. It provided just the right setting for displays of both exquisite gems and her flashing eyes. Gentlemen shoppers often became more interested in the latter than what they came to buy.

One suitor, oil millionaire Alfred T. Lucas, built her

a home that became the talk of Houston for its opulence; they married, had two children, and lived happily until his death. The widow Lucas then married a third time, to wealthy Andrew Langham. Since this union was still legally intact at the time she met Clark Gable, the Hollywood gossip mill ground out stories about how the actor "stole her away" from her less illustrious husband. This simply was not true. The Gable-Ria Langham romance was slow to develop. And Ria had had her difficulties with her third marriage even before Clark's second came upon the horizon.

Before Ria began influencing his style, Clark had taken to wearing a derby and carrying a gold-headed cane. He had cultivated the neat little mustache that was to become a hallmark, and displayed gleaming teeth in a wide smile (although they were yet to carry new caps cemented on in a dentist's chair). But his budget felt the strain of months of unemployment, and Gable often had to fend off hunger with 65-cent Italian dinners at West Side Manhattan bistros. His evenings often were spent at night court—admission free—to watch justice meted out to stickup men and prostitutes.

His wanderlust got the best of him after a jobless winter, and he headed for the West Coast for one more fling at Hollywood. Gable discovered Nancy Caroll aboard the train, and they planned to stopover in Chicago to break up the trip. "We arrived in Chicago on February fifteenth," Nancy explained, "and read in the papers of the St. Valentine's Day Massacre, in which seven members of the Bugs Moran gang had been executed by rival mobsters dressed in police uniforms. The dragnet was out, the newspapers said, for every gangster in Chicago, including Al Capone. Gable and I simultaneously had the idea of seeing the roundup, if we could."

It was his graduation from night court, and he sold Nancy on the idea of observing the action in a Chicago precinct headquarters as a way of "studying raw life, to better be able to portray it." It became, however, no more than a flash of vicariousness. They saw less then they expected: the interrogation of six frightened Negro youths arrested as murder suspects. The kids were terrified, the police unsubtle in their methods. The theatrical duo soon scrambled aboard another train headed for the Coast. It brought Gable no new film work, and he soon made the return trip to Broadway.

Gable experienced a great deal of luck, both good and bad, back in New York. He was given the leading role in *Gambling,* a new George M. Cohan production, but Gable's performance during its Philadelphia tour was sub-par and he was fired. Before Gable had too much chance to pout, however, he connected with a role in *Hawk Island,* another mystery, which brought a *Times* comment: "The principal player is Clark Gable. He is fully equal to the demands that [director Howard Irving] Young puts upon him." Howard Barnes, then with the *Tribune,* termed him "the most competent in the cast." But the play ran just twenty-four performances.

Gable's next, *Blind Windows,* had an even shorter run. He had developed a new optimism, however, which proved essential in his struggles through those dark days. "I couldn't get a job," he said about the weeks following *Blind Windows.* "But at least I could see other actors at work and study their techniques. I bought cheap balcony seats for *Journey's End* and Francine Larrimore's *Let Us Be Gay*. Katharine Cornell was playing in *Dishonored Lady*, Constance Collier in *The Matriarch*. All that winter I was on the outside looking in."

Gable was to appear for the last time as a Broadway actor in the spring of 1930, in *Love, Honor and Obey*. He had a smaller role than two other performers destined for Hollywood success—George Brent and Glenda Farrell. But as that play closed, after eight weeks, a wire from Louis O. MacLoon offered him a Los Angeles stage role as Killer Mears in *The Last Mile* and finally provided a breakthrough from oblivion. Of course, there was no way for Gable to have known it at the time. In fact, his confidence had been so shaken by a string of failures on Broadway that he hesitated to travel west and take the role. For one thing, he remembered Spencer Tracy's brilliance in playing the part in a film version. "You won't have to be that good out here," MacLoon assured him over the transcontinental telephone wires.

Gable's performance, in Los Angeles' Majestic Theater, brought rave notices and the attention of a new breed of Hollywood talent scouts. Talkies were moving in to displace the old silent films, and a host of fallen screen idols were seeing their stars removed from dressing-room doors. Talent-seekers simply had to find new stars to replace the old ones, victimized by high-pitched voices. Among them were such luminaries as John Gilbert and William Haines.

"I think you're a good bet for pictures," Lionel Barrymore told Gable upon seeing him act at the Majestic. "I want to arrange a screen test for you at my studio." It was Metro-Goldwyn-Mayer. Gable was eventually to sign with that studio, and to springboard to stardom with M-G-M.

He once told a magazine interviewer about his first day on a Metro set. Displaying his curly head to the reporter, he said sardonically: "You can see how much I need a curl, but they curled it anyhow. Then I went over to wardrobe, where they stripped me and gave me a G-string. The sound stage where they were making the test was a long way off. I'm no exhibitionist, and I was embarrassed to make that trek. When I showed up on that sound stage, I asked Lionel, 'What is this? Why am I curly-haired and half-naked?'

"I'm directing *The Bird of Paradise*,' he told me. 'I want you to play the native boy in it.' A prop man stuck a hibiscus behind one of my ears, shoved a knife in my G-string, and there I was, creeping through the bushes, looking for a girl. Lionel had made a big thing out of these actors who can't talk.' But he'd given me nothing to say throughout the test. Then my test was sent in for Irving Thalberg to look at. He called Lionel in and said, 'You can't put this man in a picture. Look at him!'

"Lionel said loyally, 'He's a good stage actor. He's young, but he'll be all right.' Irving said, 'Not for my money, he won't. Look at his big, batlike ears.' Fortunately, a woman agent had seen me and believed in me enough to sell me to Pathé for a while. Then I was at Warner's for a spell and, in December 1930, I came back to M-G-M."

The Thalberg remark gained wide publicity in time and helped build a long-standing fable about Gable's ears: that the studio had them pinned back for his early screen roles. Years later, his last wife, Kay, debunked that by explaining: "He weighed only a hundred and fifty pounds then. When you're that slim your ears can look like handles." The legend also brought with it one of the more celebrated wisecracks from the film community; Milton Berle quipped that Gable rated an award for his "best ears of our lives."

The "spell" Gable mentioned with Warner's involved a bit part opposite Barbara Stanwyck in *Night Nurse* and was followed by a Pathé role in a western. Gable had one problem in accepting a contract for the horse opera, and he confessed to his agent, Minna Wallis (sister of famed producer Hal Wallis), that he couldn't ride. "Then take lessons," commanded Miss Wallis matter-of-factly.

The deal for *The Painted Desert* was set for $750 a week. Before reporting, Gable secretly wandered into the barren country outside of Los Angeles to take riding lessons from cowboy Art Wilson. When the first day of shooting arrived, Gable was saddle-sore but ready.

But when the completed film was in the can, Gable learned from a trade newspaper that Pathé was on the verge of bankruptcy and that the release of its films was being held up. Gable knew that he could have used the exposure to a film-going public. He wondered once again if he would ever make it as an actor. And one more trial, with Warner Brothers, brought more despair. He overheard Jack Warner react to his screen test: "Why do you throw $500 of our money on a test for that big ape?" Warner bellowed at his son-in-law, Mervyn LeRoy. "Didn't you see those big ears when you talked to him? And those big feet and hands, not to mention that ugly face of his?"

But M-G-M saw Gable's potential and signed him for

a two-year $350-a-week contract, with six-month options. For the first time as an actor, Gable was assured of steady income for more than a few weeks at a time. It was December, 1930. A star, if not born, was in its embryonic stage; Gable's first role was indeed modest. He appeared as a milkman in *The Easiest Way*, opposite Constance Bennett.

Ria Langham, meantime, had arrived for a winter in California and more and more became a constant Gable companion. She consoled him through his difficulties, both emotionally and with financial help. And Gable used some of the money to have his teeth capped, against the day when a close-up camera might inhibit his potential.

His small role in *The Easiest Way* caught the attention of Joan Crawford, who asked that he play opposite her in *Dance Fools Dance*, a performance that brought Gable praise from *The New York Times*. It termed his portrayal of a gangster "a vivid and authentic piece of acting." Gable also earned new status at the studio; he had his own dressing room and sat for his first studio publicity portraits. Fan mail began trickling in for Gable.

Within a year, he was to appear in *The Secret Six* with Jean Harlow, in *A Free Soul* with Norma Shearer, opposite Marion Davies in *Polly of the Circus*, and in *Susan Lennox*, starring Greta Garbo. In all, he made twelve films in 1931 and earned this rave notice from *The Hollywood Reporter*: "A star in the making has been made. A star that, to our reckoning, will outdraw every other star pictures has developed. Never have we seen audiences work themselves into such enthusiasm as when Gable walks on the screen."

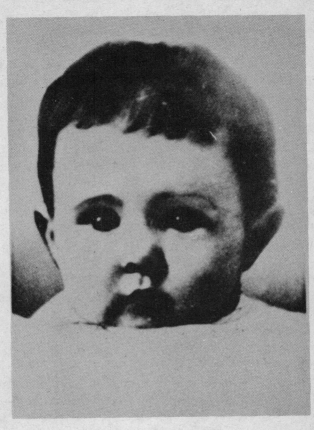

Clark Gable at six months.

Clark Gable as a boy.

Clark Gable at the beginning of his movie career.

Clark Gable, 1932.

Clark Gable and Ria Langham.

Clark Gable and Jean Harlow.

Clark Gable and Marion Davies at a costume party.

The prophecy, written by W. R. Wilkerson and published on July 13, 1931, brought little comfort to Gable, who once again felt insecurity roll over him. The shock waves of the stock market crash were depressing the motion-picture industry, as they were affecting the entire economy. Gable was nearing thirty, and since his active year was followed by ennui, he once more felt pangs of doubt.

Without financial help from Ria Langham at the time, he may not have been able to stay with his Hollywood career. Intimates knew that he was planning to marry her. Yet, before a date was set, the woman who seemed destined to weave her way in and out of his early years once again appeared. Franz Doerfler had left San Francisco to move in with two roommates and search for a dancing or acting role in films. She ran across Gable accidentally, and they once more began spending some time together. She was, Gable told her, "the only friend I have in this town." But he made no reference to her about Ria.

When Franz asked why he broke up his marriage with Josephine Dillon, Gable explained: "Josephine sure helped me a lot in my work. But she couldn't stop playing teacher. She was too domineering. You wouldn't believe it, Franz, but she acted like a Mrs. God. Anyway, I can't stand being around any woman for months at a time."

And when he began working with Constance Bennett in *The Easiest Way,* he moaned to Franz: "I don't think either Constance Bennett or the director knows I'm alive. I hate everybody at the studio, everybody I work with. And nobody at M-G-M likes me." Franz became the first to know about his new contract with M-G-M, and the first to ride in a new Ford he purchased to help celebrate the signing. But just when Franz began hoping for a new life together with Clark, he told her he was going to New York "on business." He neglected to tell her, however, what the business was: to exchange marriage vows with Ria Langham.

When the studio objected, because a bachelor Gable had more box-office sex appeal than a married star-on-the-rise, Gable indignantly not only refused to keep his marriage secret—he had the knot tied a second time, in Santa Ana, California, by Justice of the Peace Kenneth Morrison. An M-G-M publicity man served as witness. Gable was thirty years old; his bride, forty-seven.

Gable's penchant for the outdoor life developed in the early months of this marriage, as he took to hunting and fishing. He also became a family man for the first time, a stepfather of three, a husband leaning on his wife's support until he could wipe out an accumulation of debts and stand on finances he earned on his own.

If one single on-screen event propelled Gable more than any other to stardom, it was a three-foot swing of his right hand across Norma Shearer's face, during a climatic scene in *A Free Soul*. That stroke both launched his one-of-a-kind image as a man who would take no nonsense from women and a new trend for on-screen male behavior, away from the handkissing style of Rudolph Valentino. Female film-goers adored the new Gable toughness, and men envied Gable's screen mastery of Hollywood beauties. In the early thirties, audiences took their cinema far more seriously than they do today.

More recently, Norma Shearer quipped about Gable's historic slap: "Perhaps that was where Noel Coward got the idea for his line: 'Every woman should be hit regularly, like a gong.'" She also diagnosed another change in public attitudes that followed. "Gable made villains popular," she said. "Instead of the audience's wanting the good man to get the girl, they began wanting the bad man to get her."

Letter-carriers began dumping bagfuls of Gable fan mail at M-G-M, and adoring women were regularly queueing up at the studio gate for a glimpse—or a touch—of their new idol on his way home from a day's work. Yet M-G-M was slow to recognize the value of its property. It lent him to Warner's for two grade B movies. And although his weekly salary rose to $850, it was far less than the hundreds of thousands earned annually by the studio's biggest stars. The disparity annoyed his agent, Minna Wallis, and she decided to press the issue. She arranged a film contract for Gable, then tucked him away in seclusion at Palm Springs when work was scheduled to begin, and waited for her phone to ring. When the call came, she told the producer: "Of course I know where Clark is, but you won't see him until you raise his salary by a thousand dollars per week." Louis B. Mayer shouted back: "We've made Gable and we can break him twice as fast. Tell him to be in the studio at eight sharp tomorrow morning or he'll never work in Hollywood again—at this studio or any other." Gable was on time for the next day's shooting.

Turmoil surrounded him on and off the studio and he began wondering where his next role was coming from. Simultaneously, another star-in-the-making—sexpot Jean Harlow—was having her own contract difficulties. Howard Hughes was refusing to increase her $150-per-week contract, while loaning her out to other studios for ten and fifteen times her salary. The sultry blonde was becoming as much a part of the Hollywoood lexicon as was Gable. People discussed the way she fondled herself on-screen, they gossiped about her sex exploits with males she met anywhere—from taxi drivers who chanced to pick her up, to deliverymen and bellhops whom she met. Her film appearances in diaphanous gowns were much discussed, especially "behind-the-scenes" accounts of how she would rub her nipples with ice to display them better through gowns in close-up scenes.

The studio decided to cast her with fast-fading John Gilbert, in *Red Dust*, a script being written by famed New York newsman John Lee Mahin. But Mahin had other ideas. "You're crazy to use Gilbert with Harlow," he told producer Hunt Stromberg. "I just saw Gable in *The Secret Six*. He's a bull with little-boy's eyes. He can't miss." One Mahin shock scene in particular, where a cool Gable discovered a torrid Harlow bathing in a rain barrel, was too much even for the most casual movie-goer of 1932. The Gable-Harlow team was a box-office success from that scene on.

At the time, new strains began pulling at Gable's already shaky marriage with Ria. His stately wife was spending money lavishly—much of it his, as Gable's salary passed the high income level in 1933. Ria also took to ordering Gable about. "See that the Richardsons are invited to Friday's party," she would say, or "Make sure the florist sends only his best roses," or "Call the service for a butler." Ria also was selecting Gable's clothes, admonishing him for his manners, and, in general, playing mother to his growing petulance. More and more, Gable took to the seclusion of the mountains, lakes and streams, to brood on hunting trips. He stalked mountain sheep, bear and deer through the wilds of Utah, Nevada, Montana and Yellowstone Park.

Gable also became interested in Masonry, and moved up the ladder of the order after initiation in September, 1933. His film career took a new tack as well; he was cast with Carole Lombard in his first important comedy role—in *No Man of Her Own*—despite a studio suspicion that he was too strongly identified with tough roles. Gable, however, was happy to take any and all acting assignments he could get. "Clark and Carole clicked right from the start," said director Wesley Ruggles. "They make a good comedy team. One day I stopped by his dressing room to ask how things were going. Clark said he didn't think he would last long [in the film industry] and that he wanted to make hay while he could."

During the six weeks of shooting, Gable and Carole became good friends. They called each other "Maw" and "Paw," and enjoyed playing practical jokes on each other. On the final day of production, she presented him with a huge ham, decorated with his picture pinned to its flank. He returned the favor with a gift of a large, wornout pair of ballet slippers. It was his way to kid her about her dancing agility.

Gable also took a dancing role in films, in white tie and tails, with Joan Crawford and Franchot Tone. The picture, *Dancing Lady*, sparked rumors of an off-screen romance between Gable and Crawford which persisted through the years, although there appears to be little evidence of it. These rumors had Joan Crawford "carrying a torch" for Gable while, true to his film image, he would slough the matter off nonchalantly.

Dancing Lady almost prematurely marked the close of Gable's career, through a flash of his temperament. After brooding aloud over being signed to play behind Franchot Tone, he complained to M-G-M, which promptly loaned him out to Columbia for a Frank Capra movie. The studio had decided to discipline Gable by farming him out.

The Capra film, tentatively titled *Overland Bus,* was about a runaway heiress and a newspaperman traveling together from Miami to New York. Columbia Pictures then was a second-line company. Myrna Loy already had refused an offer to star in the Capra production, and when Columbia asked Louis B. Mayer for the loan of Robert Montgomery, M-G-M sent Gable instead.

"Clark came storming home upon hearing the news," Ria recalled. "He threatened to quit Metro, to walk out on his contract. I told him that if that made him happy to go ahead and do it. But I thought it would be smarter to make the movie, do his best, and see what happens." Claudette Colbert had signed on to play the female lead. Gable downed a few shots of bourbon and agreed to "try." He had serious doubts about his ability to play a comedy role. And he kept brooding about his "sell-out" through the first days of shooting.

Capra also had his doubts . . . about Gable. "He was terribly disappointed when he had to settle for Gable," explained a cameraman. "But after they talked it over, Capra came by and said. 'Don't worry. He's going to be just fine in the part.'"

Meantime, adoring flocks of women fans, lured by

Gable's growing reputation as a leading man, came to the studio courtyard. They didn't care about those stories in film magazines reporting his new role, his turn to comedy. Claudette Colbert's reaction wasn't too different, at that. "I had never met Clark," she exclaimed, "and like every woman in the country, thought he was divine. I also jumped at the gay prospect of looking at him every day—and getting paid besides!"

Although the film was being produced on a small budget ($350,000), and Capra was working his cast hard and long, Gable and Colbert managed to have a good time through the closing weeks of shooting. "We thought the picture was very funny, and Clark broke up—take after take—in some of the scenes," she said.

After that movie, M-G-M brought Gable back for undistinguished roles opposite Myrna Loy—as a doctor in *Men in White,* and once again as a gangster, in *Manhattan Melodrama.* Gable's marriage with Ria was floundering as badly as was his career. Even his agent unloaded his contract, a seemingly sure sign that the future was bleak.

In February, 1934, the Gable-Colbert comedy, retitled *It Happened One Night,* was released. Featuring such memorable scenes as a hitchhiking venture, where a pretty Colbert leg brought a car to a screeching halt, after Gable's thumbing attempts failed, and a howling display of propriety in a hotel room, where they slept on opposite sides of a dangling blanket. It was an immediate success. Overnight, the Gable mustache became widely imitated, his on-screen disdain for undershirts caused sales dips in that commodity in dry-goods stores across America, and the bus run from Miami to New

York began carrying a bevy of adventurous young ladies, each looking for a Clark Gable all their own.

Academy Awards were presented on February 27, 1935, at the Biltmore Hotel in Los Angeles. Ria persuaded Clark to attend (they were reconciled again), although he didn't want to face the prospect of seeing someone else honored. And Claudette Colbert at first planned to be elsewhere (she was certain Bette Davis would carry home the Oscar for her work in *Of Human Bondage*). But *It Happened One Night* walked off with five honors, including picture of the year, best screenplay, and best director. Claudette Colbert was feted as actress of the year. And an unbelieving Clark Gable, who hadn't wanted the role in the first place, found himself walking to center stage to accept an Oscar for actor of the year. Gable's days of worry over contracts and studio status were at last behind him, once and for all.

He was rushed into the big leagues of Hollywood incomes; only the salaries of Greta Garbo, Joan Crawford, and Wallace Beery topped the $211,553 he contracted for over the next year. Gable went on a national tour. Women mobbed the new star at New York's Capitol Theater, stealing his handkerchief, cufflinks, and wrist watch for souvenirs; twenty-five hundred of them screamed and crushed together at the train station in Kansas City; in San Francisco, and everywhere else he went, it was more of the same. Then there were the eccentric types: the girl who slipped into his elevator in Baltimore and tried to kiss him, and her counterpart in another town who slipped off her bra and demanded his autograph on it, plus scores more who wrote him to ask for "one night of love."

"Mr. Gable and I are not separated at all. We have never been and I don't think we ever will be. It is ridiculous. There has been no difficulty or disagreement between us." Thus did Ria Langham "protest too much" when reporters asked about a rumored rift in their marriage. In December, 1931, after Gable returned from an arduous personal tour of South America, he moved from his home to the Beverly Wilshire Hotel. Clark and Ria had agreed on a community property settlement—an expensive one for Gable—but he still insisted publicly that there were no plans for a divorce.

Ria confided in friends that her estranged husband had "been under tremendous pressure." "It was a combination of too much work, too sudden success and the fact that women fairly throw themselves at him all the time," she rationalized. "Basically, he had good Dutch principles, and no one could be sweeter at times. But he could be stubborn and perverse."

The break-up spurred gossip-column items which linked him with an English actress, a Long Island socialite, and Loretta Young, co-star in one of his first movies after *It Happened One Night—Call of the Wild*. Gable shrugged off the rumors. "Blame our separation on me," he said. "Mrs. Gable is a fine woman. And as for those other stories, I only dated one of those women— the Long Island girl—and that was just once, to a hockey match."

Ria and Clark endured a friendly separation; they dated occasionally, and phoned each other often. Two months after they began living apart, they attended a Jock Whitney party, the White Mayfair Ball. Norma Shearer broke tradition by appearing in a red gown (all ladies were asked to wear white). Carole Lombard,

Clark Gable and his father, William Gable, 1937.

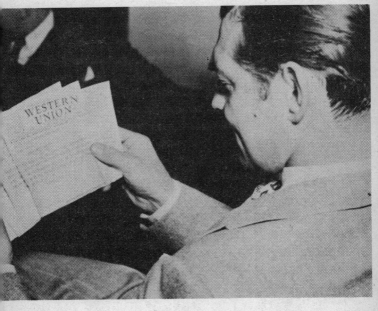

Clark Gable reading telegrams from friends during the trial of Mrs. Violet Norton, who charged him with being the father of her daughter, 1937.

Clark Gable and Claudette Colbert in a scene from "It Happened One Night."

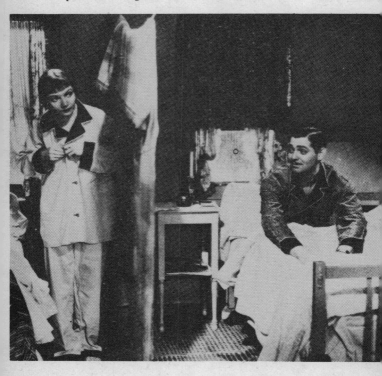

Clark Gable and Claudette Colbert in a scene from "It Hap-
ened One Night."

Clark Gable and Carole Lombard, 1939.

whom Gable hadn't seen in four years, caused a sensation by arriving in a screaming ambulance and "entering" on a stretcher, carried by two men dressed as attendants. In the time since Gable and Carole worked together, she had shed husband William Powell, but remained the same cut-up Gable enjoyed on location.

"I go for you, Maw," he told her as they whirled on the dance floor. "I go for you too, Paw," she said. "How long do you suppose it would take you to get rid of your escorts?" Gable asked. "As long as it will take for you to get rid of that woman you're with," she answered. They left immediately, and began dating each other in earnest.

Yet Gable had no interest in a renewed life as a one-woman man, even ostensibly. His dates with glamorous Merle Oberon were especially interesting to the columnists. But one gossip item that reached a column-reading public was especially galling. It reported the "real" reason for Gable's split-up with Ria. Her daughter, George Anna, had been married the year before to a Houston doctor and gave birth to a son in February, 1936. Gable, the columnist said, left Ria because he had no interest in being identified as a grandfather!"

If the gossip-mongers were annoying, they were tolerated as a necessary evil in stardom; he followed *China Seas,* with Jean Harlow, with the role of Fletcher Christian in *Mutiny on the Bounty*—although it was a part he didn't particularly relish (he felt the casting of Charles Laughton and Franchot Tone relegated him to third fiddle). And besides, the part called for Gable to shave his mustache, and he had grown fond of it. But it brought a nomination for an Academy Award, and

Gable always said that it was one of the most enjoyable parts he ever played.

In *San Francisco*, a fight scene with Spencer Tracy and Clark Gable helped advance Tracy's ascendancy to stardom; that picture followed Gable's performance in *Wife versus Secretary*, in which Harlow and Myrna Loy completed a triangle. Yet Gable's omnipresent insecurity again prevailed through his next two films: *Cain and Mabel* and *Love on the Run*. Neither were box-office smashes, and Gable wondered if his luck was about to run out. He felt a bit better about things on January 20, 1937, when he was "immortalized" in Hollywood's traditional cementprint ceremony at Grauman's Chinese Theater. Gable honored the theater's owner with a caption: "To Sid, Who is a Great Guy," as he pressed his footprints in fresh cement before a record-breaking crowd. No larger group was to watch a Grauman ceremony for twenty-four years, until Doris Day was feted.

In April, 1937, Franz Doerfler again came into his life—for the last time—on the wings of a subpoena. She was a key witness in a scandalous trial. Years later, Gable related the events this way:

"I got a letter or two, at my home, from a woman in Canada. She asked me if she could see me about a personal matter. I didn't know her. In fact, I had never heard of her, so I ignored her. But her letters kept arriving just the same. She finally said I would remember her because she had been in England in such and such a year, that I'd had an affair with her then and, as a result, a child had been born. Her letters said something should be done about providing for the child.

"At the time she said all this happened," Gable continued, "I'd never been in England. I'd never been out of North America—so I'd never had a United States passport. As affairs go, the one she described was a long-distance project. It must have set a world's record so I decided she was nuts and forgot about it. Then Walter Winchell began to get letters from her about me, and another columnist, Jimmy Fiddler, got letters too. And letters also began to arrive at my studio, M-G-M, and Fiddler and Winchell and the studio asked, 'What's all this?'

"I was told by the United States district attorney in Los Angeles that his office had heard about those letters, and he sent an assistant United States district attorney to see me. He told me, 'You'll not only have to prove that you weren't in England when this child was conceived you'll have to prove where you actually were at that time. Can you?' I replied that it wouldn't be easy. When the woman who wrote those letters said I was in England, I was pretty much a wandering trouper. I was in and out of shows and working in lumber camps. But I came up with two kinds of proof: old, dated theater programs with my name on them, and checks made out to me by the Silverton Lumber Company, Silverton, Oregon."

Postal authorities indicted the woman, Violet Norton, for using the mails to defraud. Headlines screamed the trial news across the nation, as federal judge George Cosgrave convened his court on April 22, 1937. An all-male jury heard the evidence above the tumult of women battling for available seats in the crowded courtroom. Scores more of them milled about outside, waiting to see the principals involved, especially Gable.

Star witness Franz Doerfler told of her romance with

Gable and their life in Oregon. The trial even brought a reconciliation between Gable and his father, who came to testify that Clark was born and bred in the United States and that "there have been Gables in this country for four hundred years."

The jury returned a verdict of guilty, which was reversed five days later. An appellate court ruled that mail fraud was an improper charge, that the charge should have been extortion or attempted blackmail. Violet Norton was deported to Canada on February 7, 1938, and was ordered to stay out of the United States for a year.

Gable returned to film work and took up some activities for side income. Radio was a prime medium in the late thirties, and Gable demanded—and got—$7,500 for single on-air appearances (although a ceiling of $5,000 was universal in the broadcast industry). But he had little stomach for merchandising his career on the airwaves and made his last appearance for several years in March, 1939, with Claudette Colbert, in a re-creation of *It Happened One Night.*

Love on the Run, Gable's next film, was a colossal flop. He portrayed Charles Parnell, the Irish patriot in the film *Parnell,* a version of Ireland's battle for home rule. Gable affected an Irish accent for the role, grew long sideburns, and let his mustache grow full. After the film's release, M-G-M opened bushels of fan mail about its prize male property—almost all of it indignant. "Let others portray historical figures," read a typical letter. "Gable is cut out for roles where he gets tough with women. That's what he's good at, and that's what I'll pay to see." Gable took a large dose of good-natured ribbing from his friends (including Carole Lombard, whom he now was dating heavily and who would, years later, continue to kid him about that flop by placing "Parnell" publicity stickers behind his ties, in books he was reading, under bread at his dinner table, and so on.) At the time, however, *Love on the Run* provided a lesson. "No one is ever going to sell me a bill of goods again," he told friends. "I know my limitations and I really am at my best in an open shirt, blue jeans and boots."

Saratoga, featuring the tried-and-true tough-guy Gable, restored his standing with his fans. During its filming, co-star Jean Harlow died, and the studio decided to complete Harlow's role with an understudy who looked like her from the rear. Mary Dees, the Harlow look-alike, worked the rest of the film with her back to the camera, and she and Gable became such good friends that he asked for parts for her in many of his pictures that followed.

The Gable build-up continued in the fall of 1938 when columnist Ed Sullivan decided to run a "King and Queen of Hollywood" contest in the fifty-five syndicated papers where his column appeared. After twenty million ballots were counted, Gable and Myrna Loy were declared the winners and were "coronated" in a much-publicized ceremony. From that day, the nickname "King" stuck with Gable—although it was more apt to be used by those who were not his closest friends.

"King" Gable and "Queen" Myrna Loy were teamed together in *Test Pilot;* they shared billing with Spencer Tracy and Lionel Barrymore, and appeared together again in a clinker, *Too Hot to Handle.* The latter caused more excitement during its filming than after. A controlled fire on location got out of hand, and the studio cameras kept grinding as Gable performed a real-life rescue of Myrna Loy.

While the studio busily projected its "King and Queen" team on-screen, his off-camera romance with Carole Lombard was developing splendidly. On Christmas Day, 1938, Gable gave Carole two gifts—a huge plaster statue of the actress, which she characteristically liked very much, but came to use as a hatrack, and a spanking new, shiny yellow Cadillac convertible.

Before Carole Lombard entered his life, Gable explained his first two marriages, to older women, this way: "The older woman has seen more, heard more and knows more than the demure young woman with the pretty face and shapely figure. I'll take the older woman every time." But Carole Lombard, twenty-seven and endowed with a pretty face and shapely figure, knew her way around. Two months after Gable's display of Christmas generosity to her, he divorced Ria Langham. And less than a month after that, Carole Lombard became the third Mrs. Gable.

CHAPTER 4

*Love, Lombard,
and the
War Years*

It has been said that Clark Gable liked his women two ways—sacred and profane. Carole Lombard provided him with a perfect blend; the idol of her time in films, she could match the vilest tongue on any Hollywood set. Yet she could wriggle into the highly feminine dress of her era and dazzle the most sophisticated of men. Some believe that to the time of his final marriage, to Kay Spreckles, Gable experienced love only once before—with Carole Lombard.

An Indianapolis *News* reporter once summed her up this way: "She looks New Yorkish, talks Bostonish, and acts very Londonish. In manner, she is brisk and slangy —an attitude which belies her fragile type of beauty." She also loved to toss off a "kiss my ass" to producers who were rough with her or who pawed her. And one particular flash of Lombard temperament is remembered more than any other; the time she stormed onto a set where Gable was working to tell the director: "Get that whore out of this film or Gable goes." It seems that the "other girl" had been trying to bed her Clark. The girl was fired.

At five-foot-one and 112 pounds packed curvaceously under light, naturally blond hair, she was feminine, intelligent, and athletic. She also was one of Hollywood's most superb scene stealers, and more than one actor objected to her insistence on the employment of cameraman Teddy Tezlaff for all her movies. It seems that Tezlaff knew how to line Carole up for more than her share of flattering camera angles.

When Carole entered the world—as Jane Peters—in Fort Wayne, Indiana, on October 6, 1909, there was little thought in the family household that, in fifteen years, she would be starred opposite Edmund Lowe in a film, *Marriage in Transit.* (To create her stage name, she took "Carole" from a ten-cent astrology booklet, and "Lombard" from the name of a neighbor, a retired banker.)

The Peters family was wealthy and industrious; grandfather John founded the Horton Company in Fort Wayne, after importing the first washing machine to the United States from Germany, and his son Frederick, (Carole's father) spurred the company's growth as its vice-president. On her mother's (Cheney) side, a great-grandfather established one of the first electric companies in California and helped finance the laying of the Atlantic cable. He also was a director on the first board of New York's National City Bank.

Elizabeth K. Peters separated from Frederick when Carole was seven and took the girl and her two older brothers to California. Four years later, director Alan Dwayn found himself absorbed in the antics of a high-spirited tomboy cavorting on his front lawn. He put her in his newest movie, *The Perfect Crime,* and Carole found the experience so enjoyable that she became a dropout as soon as the school year, her tenth, was finished.

Carole's facility on horseback brought early roles in westerns. Hollywood legend also has it that these pictures developed her salty language; horse-opera extras were reputed to have the industry's bluest tongues. She often startled them with her use of four-letter comebacks when the lechers went too far during off-camera advances. Carole's perfect features and look of innocence belied her toughness.

She also seemed destined for tragedy. Carole suffered a deep nose-to-cheekbone gash in an auto accident before she was twenty. After receiving twenty stitches, she was assured by doctors that her scar would gradually fade away. But it was deep enough for a long enough time to warrant close-up shooting only from Carole's other side.

After a nine-month sabbatical from the cameras, Carole bounced back from the accident with work in Mack Sennett comedies and soon became known as one of Hollywood's most gifted comediennes. Before she was thirty, she became the highest-paid actress of them all, demanding—and receiving—$150,000 a picture, with percentage deals thrown in.

Her marriage to William Powell had suffered from the seventeen-year gap between their ages; they wed when she was twenty-one. But Gable was another matter; she *wanted* that marriage to work, and worked at it through the five exciting years they shared. When she learned Clark didn't like night life, she gave up the owlish schedule she adored. And the sharing of his love for the outdoors involved a tremendous effort. Although

Clark Gable hunting in Mexico, 1940.

Clark Gable serving with the U.S. 8th Army Air Force in England, 1943.

Captain Clark Gable, U.S. 8th Army Air Force, 1943.

Clark Gable and Gary Cooper hunting at Sun Valley, Idaho, 1945.

Clark Gable and model Anita Colby, 1948.

Clark Gable and actress Paulette Goddard, 1948.

Clark Gable and Sylvia Ashley honeymooning in Honolulu, 1950.

Carole was an adroit rider and sportswoman, she was really most at home in the comforts of *her* home.

Yet the Gable-Lombard match could be fiery, even before it became a marriage, as Gable biographer Charles Samuels reported in *The King*. "There was one night she couldn't sleep," Samuels wrote. "Waking up at three in the morning, she picked up a fan magazine. In it was an interview with her beloved. He was quoted as saying that girls chased him despite all he could do to calm them down.

"Carole punched the pillow, ripped the sheets and began screeching like a famished eaglet. She grabbed for the phone, got Clark on the line, and read the riot act to him:

" 'Our engagement is off, you son of a bitch. Here is one dame who isn't chasing you.' "

According to Samuels, Gable also ignited her temper with boasts of his skills between the sheets, ribald tales of love-making that included exploits in a canoe, a telephone booth, and on a fire escape. "I even did it in a swimming pool," he once bragged to Carole. "You know, it's hard to do under water." This time, Carole tried a different reaction. "Yes, isn't it?" she replied sweetly. Whereupon Gable bellowed in full cry: "What kind of girl are you? Doing a thing like that and then having the nerve to boast to me about it!"

According to one Hollywood source, perhaps Gable's most elegant rebuff was many more years in the making. In the late fifties, while staying in a fashionable New York hotel, he is said to have been startled by a chambermaid who entered his room while he was still in bed. "Take off your clothes and join me," he offered, with that quizzical half smile she probably had seen many times before on a neighborhood movie screen. "How much will you pay me?" she asked. "Why, my dear, I would think you would want to sleep with me just to be able to say you did so," he said coolly. But she insisted on some money, and walked out to wait till he left so she could make up the room.

Late in 1938, as the Gable-Lombard "engagement" was approaching its third anniversary, *Photoplay* magazine featured "Hollywood's Unmarried Wives and Husbands," an "exposé" of eight such unions. The lead paragraphs read:

"To the outside world Clark Gable and Carole Lombard might as well be married. So might Bob Taylor and Barbara Stanwyck. Or George Raft and a minor actress, Charlie Chaplin and Paulette Goddard. Unwed couples they might be termed. But they go everywhere together; do everything in pairs. No hostess would think of inviting them separately, or pairing them with another. They solve one another's problems, handle each other's business affairs.

"They build houses near each other, buy land in bunches, take up each other's hobbies, father or mother each other's children—even correct each other's clothes—each other's personalities! Yet to the world, their official status is just friends."

The article went on to gossip about the strange gifts Clark and Carole exchanged, and her sacrifices to make their lives together compatible. "But her name is still Carole Lombard," the piece admonished. "Usually, something formidable stands in the way of a marriage certificate when Hollywood stars pair up minus a preacher. In Clark and Carole's case, of course, there is a very sound legal barrier. Clark is still officially a married man. Every now and then negotiations for a divorce are started, but, until something happens in court, Ria Gable is still the only wife the law of the land allows Clark Gable."

The article touched off mass buying of that issue of *Photoplay* and raised more than eyebrows at the then powerful Hayes office. Various studios ordered the exposed stars to marry. (All did, eventually, except for George Raft. His "fiancée," a Catholic, refused to remarry for religious reasons.) The subsequent rush to the altar by Gable was reported to have cost him a half million dollars in settlements with Ria Langham.

He married Carole on March 29, 1939, at the First Methodist Episcopal Church in Kingman, Arizona, during his first day off from shooting on the set of *Gone with the Wind.*

The studio had announced his signing for the film the August before, after a survey of moviegoers showed overwhelming sentiment for Gable as its Rhett Butler. It seems that in wading through the runaway best-selling book version, many readers fixed Gable in their mind's eye for a possible movie rendition. The man himself was certain of his chances for success with the role.

As he once explained: "It seemed that the public's casting was being guided by an elaborate publicity campaign. That novel was one of the all-time best-sellers. People didn't just read it, they lived it. They visualized its characters, and they formed passionate convictions about them . . . they had a preconceived idea of the kind of Rhett Butler they were going to see, and suppose I came up empty?"

Elaborate, widely publicized polls also favored Bette

Davis and Margaret Sullavan as runaway choices for the role of Scarlett O'Hara. But producer David O. Selznick, his heart and checkbook set on a Hollywood newcomer, was mulling other prospects over, Joan Fontaine, Lana Turner, Susan Hayward, and Lucille Ball among them, until he saw screenings of a little-known English girl—Vivien Leigh. He offered her the role and announced her signing in December, a month before work began on the film.

Selznick had just signed a three-year contract of his own, assigning distribution rights for his films to United Artists. He was forced into an expensive deal to secure the services of Clark Gable for *Gone with the Wind*. Louis B. Mayer insisted on a clause to move the film's distribution through Loew's Inc., M-G-M's parent company; terms called for an estimated payment by Selznick of $25 million for Gable's involvement alone. (With each revival, *Gone with the Wind* has become one of the most profitable movies in film history. But Clark Gable—and his heirs—have never received a dime above his original contract.)

Although destined for this kind of success, the film was slow in progressing. Gable grumbled over an ill-fitting wardrobe. "It was the only time I saw Clark angry," said one observer. "There he was, knocking himself out to make the character perfect and the clothes were terrible." Selznick solved the problem by calling in a noted Hollywood tailor. It was the smallest of several problems plaguing the film.

Gable objected to working under George Cukor, whom he felt was a "woman's director." The star thought Vivien Leigh would come off too well, at his expense, dropping Rhett Butler to second-class status. Gable suggested Victor Fleming be retained, and Fleming replaced Cukor after the first week.

Gable also objected to playing a scene which called for him to weep at the news of Scarlett's miscarriage. That argument lasted until Selznick offered a compromise; the scene would be shot both ways, with and without the self-pity. Gable eventually agreed that the original version was best.

In time, work moved steadily and the crew managed to lighten a rugged pace with some practical jokes. One of the more celebrated came during the shooting of a scene where Rhett Butler manfully carries Scarlett up a winding staircase. Vivien Leigh was a prime perpetrator of the gag; she kept murmuring that a different flaw was spoiling each take and insisted on "just one more" through a dozen retakes. Gable, exhausted, was set to call it a day, when Fleming admitted: "The first take was perfect, Clark. The others were just for laughs."

Gable took that one graciously enough, but was less patient with Vivien Leigh's lack of punctuality. Toward the end of their work, they were scheduled to shoot publicity stills late one morning. As ever, Gable was on time, but Vivien was not. And Gable knew that her delays for this particular stint compounded his wait; the process of dressing her in the elaborate period costume for the film and making her up was long, indeed. When he became especially edgy as the minutes ticked away, Gable was told that Vivien had arrived in makeup. But studio hands knew that she had not. Gable walked angrily off an hour later, after looking for himself and finding that she still had not arrived. Then came Vivien's turn for a flash of temper. An hour later, when she showed up, she learned that Clark hadn't waited for her.

Once the film was in the can, the studio moved forward with exploitation plans. "The biggest news event since Sherman," hailed the Atlanta *Constitution* when *Gone with the Wind* premiered there on December 15, 1939. The event brought an entourage to the southern city which, less than a century before, had experienced the ravages of the Civil War depicted in the film. Georgia's governor helped magnify the event by declaring a state holiday, and the city administration extended the celebration for two more days. Revelry carried into the early hours with period costume balls, receptions, and a sustaining carnival atmosphere.

It all began when an American Airlines plane, *Gone with the Wind* painted on its fuselage, brought Clark and Carole to a wild airport reception. A second airliner brought Selznick, Vivien Leigh and Laurence Olivier (her husband at the time), and Olivia de Havilland. An open-car motorcade through the seven miles of road connecting Atlanta and its airport evoked hysteria from rows of fans lining the way. Two thousand more paid ten dollars a ticket for the premiere, filling the Grand Theater, as the Mayor reported that 38,000 more requests had to be turned back after all seats were sold. Another 8,000 tickets, at $10 each, admitted celebrants to a Junior League Ball on the following night. Then too, there were numerous daytime receptions and teas.

In the theater, the audience gasped through the scene where Gable snarls at Leigh: "Frankly, my dear, I don't give a damn." (It was an unprecedented use of what then was a taboo swear word.) *Film Daily* reviewed *GWTW* as the "mightiest achievement in the history of the motion picture. Clark Gable and Vivien Leigh are certain for this year's top awards."

The statement was two thirds accurate. *Gone with the Wind* continues to add new successes, even today. And her work in the film won the 1939 Academy Award as Actress of the Year for Vivien Leigh. Gable, although nominated for the best actor award, did not win. But the film swept seven more academy awards: Picture of the Year; Best Supporting Actress (Hattie McDaniel, as Mammy); Best Director (Fleming); Best Written Screenplay (by Sidney Howard); Best Color Cinematography; Best Art Direction, and Best Film Editing.

Gable, who insisted on four-month vacations after completing his pictures, settled down to blissful married life with Carole Lombard after this one. They had just finished furnishing a sumptuous, eight-room ranch house in Encino, California, situated on twenty acres. Its white brick exterior and eggshell white interiors had the effect of extending the sunny days of southern California by reflecting the light at sunset. And the property brought a renewed interest to Clark in farming.

Gable sought to make the ranch self-sustaining; he delved through agricultural journals to seek the newest ways to develop his land. Most mornings, he could be seen riding about on a small yellow tractor, his favorite farm toy. It brought Gable even more joy than did the road scraper he loved to operate from time to time.

Gable added 125 citrus trees to the 250 that were on his land and carefully sprayed whitewash on them and on the fences ringing the property. The home itself, however, became Carole's responsibility. She even submerged a profitable movie career to make their house a home; Carole told her agent she would consider only contracts which called for work at times that Clark was under contract.

If Clark and Carole divided tasks between indoor and outdoor operations, they arranged to enjoy the outdoor part of their life together. Carole learned to shoot a .22-caliber rifle, selected a wardrobe of fitted sports clothes, bound her hair up in pigtails during daylight hours, and often took to the hills with Clark on hunting, fishing, and camping expeditions aboard a custom-built Dodge truck with four-wheeled drive and a special sleeping compartment. They purchased hand-made saddles for riding; Gable's favorite in the stable was a show horse named Sonny, while Carole favored Melody, a bay polo pony. A time came, however, when Carole had little taste for riding; she felt a consuming yen for motherhood (that wasn't to be satisfied).

Gable's animal population at the time included several dogs, among them Bobby, a short-haired German pointer, an excellent hunting dog; Commissioner, a perky dachshund; and watchdog Tuffy, a boxer. But Tuffy, as it turned out, was not the best of watchdogs.

Gable described at length to a magazine interviewer an anecdote that included his disenchantment with Tuffy: "One morning, between nine and ten, I went out to dig ditches in the orchard. A ring on my finger was too tight, so I went back to the house to get rid of the ring and pick up a pair of smokes. As I pushed the ring off in my dressing room, there were mirrors behind me and before me. Behind me, I saw a door open slowly. A foot came out, then a hat brim. And a guy stepped out with one hand in his pocket. He wasn't facing me, so he didn't see me."

Perhaps it was the "tough guy" roles he so often played and rehearsed hour upon hour that drove Gable to instinctive action. As he explained: "I let him have it behind the ear; he went down, with me on top of him. I was after the hand he had in his pocket. When I got it out, the hand had one of my own guns in it. I took it away and tossed it into a corner. 'Get downstairs,' I told him, but he was inclined to be stubborn about it. I grabbed him by his collar and said, 'If you won't walk, you'll have to go the other way,' and I dragged him down the stairs and into the kitchen. It was a bouncy drag."

Although there were servants immediately outside the house, the scuffle went unnoticed, and Gable looked at his intruder to find him little more than a kid. "He didn't look more than twenty-one," Gable said. "I pulled him to his feet in the kitchen, and asked, 'What are you doing here?' and he said, 'I wanted some money.' 'You have a peculiar way of asking for it,' I told him. 'There are better ways.'

"I didn't know it then, but he had been there the night before, peering through my windows. He'd looked through my gun-room window, he'd seen my guns, and seeing them had swelled his larceny gland. But I didn't think he was a professional stickup man, so I said, 'You shouldn't be doing things like this. Aren't you sorry?' He said, 'No, I'm not sorry.' "

That admission changed Gable's first impulse toward leniency. " 'Oh . . . so,' he said to the youngster, 'that puts a different light on it.' He made a lunge for the door, and this time I tackled him the way an end tackles a halfback. Then I called the police and they took him away.

Clark Gable and Kay W. Spreckles after their elopement at Minden, Nevada, July 11, 1955.

Clark Gable, Gene Barry and Michael Rennie during the filming of "Soldier of Fortune," Hong Kong, 1955.

Clark Gable hunting at Gila Bend, Arizona, 1958.

Clark Gable, 1960.

Mrs. Kay Gable leaving Church of the Recessional at Forest Lawn Memorial Park, Glendale, California, after the funeral of her husband, Clark Gable, November 19, 1960.

Josephine Dillon, Clark Gable's first wife, holding her favorite photo of her former husband when she learned of his death, November 16, 1960.

*Mrs. Kay Gable and her two-week-old son, John Clark Gable,
born after the death of Clark Gable.*

"I had to appear against him," Gable said. "I don't know what happened to him after that. If he had shown any signs of remorse, I wouldn't have called the cops, but when I asked him if he was sorry, he just kept saying 'No' in a sulky way."

Where does Tuffy fit in? Gable offered it as an afterthought: "That story has a funny angle. I had a boxer watchdog guarding my place. Later on, I found out that the robber and my dog had slept in my automobile in my garage the previous night. After that, I called my watchdog Old Dependable." But Old Dependable—nee Tuffy—stayed on as the family watchdog just the same.

Servants were hired and fired several times during the first months the Gables lived on the ranch, until a dependable team was established. The household staff consisted of a caretaker and his wife, a cook, a maid, and a butler-valet. Evenings, Carole set casual mood and attire aside, let her hair fall free down her back, and donned soft gowns that looked more like what she wore in films. Yet most of the Gables' entertaining was casual—usually friends over for dinner and quiet conversation.

Those who arrived for the first time were taken through the house by Gable. Not averse to using clichés, he called it his "fifty-cent tour." And Carole, who also had a way with the tired phrase, more often than not would say: "Careful, or he'll collect the fifty cents."

The tour began in the huge living room, which featured white-paneled woodwork, a white brick fireplace, and lush, canary-yellow wall-to-wall carpeting. Two large sofas, red quilted wing-back chairs, and large, green club chairs were strategically placed for cozy tête-à-têtes in the room, with pine coffee tables set comfortably near for drinks. A collection of polished antique pitchers glimmered through an expensive glass cabinet tucked in one corner. Across the room, a Colonial staircase led to the second floor, to the master bedroom suites and an attic storage closet for Gable's hunting gear, plus a bath and a dressing room. Carole's dressing room was a prototype for a Hollywood star; it had a white fur rug, elegant crystal and silver fixtures, and wrap-around mirrors for accessible darting looks to check her appearance from any angle.

Carole's suite, just next door, was replete with white goatskin throw rugs, a dainty four-poster bed, a white sofa and matching chairs, with drapes of chintz and organdy. The resulting soft effect was continued with tufted wallpaper.

Gable's bath displayed antique bottles, almost as many mirrors as Carole had, and closet space for the extensive wardrobe accumulated by a much-employed Hollywood star. His bedroom featured a fine old desk (a gift from Selznick after *Gone with the Wind*) and a bed made of brown tufted leather. Beige dominated the room—on quilted wallpaper and on various furniture coverings. Gable also had shelves built for the books he used as a sort of post-graduate self-improvement program, begun at the time of his marriage to Josephine Dillon.

Downstairs, the tour would proceed through a first-floor bedroom-office (for his secretary, Jean Garceau), where files, an intercom, a phone system and blue-green pieces of furniture were surrounded by yellow wallpaper and drapes. Past the white, marbled powder room, one entered Gable's pride and joy, his gun room, where hand-tooled leather cases housed a collection of hunting weapons, old pistols, and other assorted fire-arms.

A gleaming kitchen produced the steak-and-potato dinners that Gable favored. He also liked spareribs, baked beans, hamburgers, chocolate cake, and home-made ice cream. Gable was no gourmet. But if the meals were unimaginative, the service was not; Water-ford crystal and Spode adorned the dining table, an-tique silverware was set, and dinner usually was served by the soft light of kerosene lamps—genuine antiques. Exquisite linen also was set at mealtimes.

One of Gable's favorite pastimes was tinkering with automobiles. He was a fine mechanic (in fact, he often speculated that had his film career not been successful, he might have earned his keep under the hoods of cars). Gable looked after his assortment of engines in a large garage, while Carole favored the Cadillac Gable had given her one Christmas. With his wide range of inter-est in cars, he owned and drove Lincolns, Fords, Chryslers, Jaguars, and Mercedes-Benzes.

Each full day of contentment at the Encino ranch usually ended with Clark reading mystery novels in bed with soft music in the background. They were happy times for the couple, yet friends had difficulty pinpoint-ing special reasons for it. Certainly, there was Clark's rare experience at love, and Carole's determination to make the marriage work. Perhaps nothing more was in-volved.

And, contrary to a widespread item from the rumor mills of the time, sex was far from the adhesive that kept them together. Carole, who was not above dis-cussing her most intimate secrets with friends, often said that Gable had been "sex-starved for years." She also would add gratuitously: "My God, you know how much I love Paw (meaning Clark). But he's not what I'd call a good lay."

As idyllic as life had become for them, they did not fully enjoy the relaxed quietude they sought at the Encino ranch. Although located twelve miles from Hollywood and twenty from Los Angeles, the Gables were almost daily annoyed by rubber-necking movie fans who drove out in their autos, and by tour buses that rattled up to the front gate, its passengers gaping while a guide blared out facts and figures about the couple: when they were married, who they starred with in certain movies, how much they made a year, *ad nauseam*.

Things came to such a pass that Gable finally installed high fences and an electrically controlled gate, with a loudspeaker apparatus, to make sure of the identity of those who had arrived at their property.

The Gables also strived for peace against the professional demands of their studios; they set a rule that publicity pictures could be taken only on the grounds, and none inside their home.

Gable's career progressed with a starring role in *Boom Town*, a picture that combined a reunion with Claudette Colbert with a bit of personal nostalgia; its scenario dealt with the rise and fall of oilmen. (Spencer Tracy appeared in a featured role.) The work evoked bittersweet memories for Gable of younger days, and the admonitions of his father to stay and work in the fields.

That poignancy was heightened by a new, late-blooming closeness between Gable and his father; Clark had arranged for the aging gentleman to come and live nearby; he built a home on his property for his father, who lived there the remaining years of his life.

Meanwhile, the dual careers of Clark and Carole were the talk of the Hollywood community, where it was axiomatic that private and public lives of its stars were incompatible. Such marriages, the feeling was, could not, and most often didn't last. But their formula for working together and vacationing together seemed to work quite well for these stars, among Hollywood's greatest of the time.

As Gable was completing *Boom Town,* Carole was in the midst of an assignment with RKO, in *They Knew What They Wanted.* When fan mail suggested that pairing Gable with Hedy Lamarr would spell financial success (as it did for them in *Boom Town,* although she had less than top billing), the two were paired in *Comrade X*—and Carole signed on for *Mr. and Mrs. Smith,* directed by Alfred Hitchcock.

The happy Gable marriage became so much a legend in Hollywood that movie colony couples sought them out for advice when their own domestic problems became a burden. Did the Gables have anything worthwhile to impart? One anecdote suggests they did not.

One evening, while at a dinner party hosted by the Alfred Hitchcocks, Mrs. H. took Carole aside and explained that recently, after twelve years of mostly happy marriage, the Hitchcocks took to quarreling. The situation, Mrs. Hitchcock said, was worsening. After some thought, Carole related the following story: Before their marriage, Gable had once given Carole a shrunken head as a good-luck charm. A time came, Carole explained, when *they* began quarreling, and Carole hoped to reverse the trend while out driving with Gable one night. Believing that the shrunken head had something to do with their problems, Carole asked Clark to stop the car on a mountain road. After pulling the head from her handbag, she ceremoniously dispatched it into the canyon below. Carole explained to the startled Gable that the head "must have had some curse on it," and that it was the source of their difficulties.

Hours and a few drinks later, Gable expressed worry that the "police might find the head, with our fingerprints on it." The couple drove to the canyon to search for it by flashlight. Carole explained about the "curse" to police who came to see who was prowling about. The officers were at first awed to find Hollywood's best-known couple groveling in the dirt in search of an Indian shrunken head. And the police recovered their aplomb soon enough to aid in the search, with one of them finding the head.

Carole explained to Mrs. Hitchcock that they decided to bury the head, but not on their own grounds. The punch line of the story, told to an astonished hostess: the Gables drove to the very grounds of the house they were in that evening (before the Hitchcocks rented it). "We put a curse on your marriage by burying it here," Carole said, in all seriousness.

The Gables had other flights into infantile behavior, especially when they teamed up for their most common practical joke—at the expense of friends who were less than close. There were times when a foursome would sit soberly through dinner at Encino while the hosts casually would throw out every vulgarity, such as spicing up a "Please pass the salt" with a fourletter adjective.

Early in 1941, an old shoulder injury, acquired while filming *San Francisco* five years earlier, began bothering Gable anew; he decided upon treatment at Johns Hopkins in Baltimore. Carole accompanied him. After learning about massages and exercises to be followed, they took a side trip to Washington, climaxed by a visit to the White House. President Franklin D. Roosevelt had learned that the Gables were in Washington and, as he said upon greeting them, Roosevelt was especially happy to meet Carole.

The President recalled seeing a news story in 1938, headlined "Carole Lombard Is Glad U.S. Takes Most of Pay," an account which quoted Carole as saying: "The government spent most of the rest of my year's earnings on general improvements for the country, and I really think I got my money's worth." The article explained the "rest" of her earnings as 85 per cent of the $465,000 she earned for the year. (She retained about $20,000 of the amount, after taxes, expenses and contributions.) The account was widely disseminated and brought bales of favorable fan mail to Carole and, as she learned that day in Washington, the President's approval as well.

Months later, on the day after the Japanese attacked Pearl Harbor, Carole wrote to the President asking how the Gables might best serve the country. A return letter signed by Roosevelt suggested that for the time being they should just continue entertaining the public. But weeks later, a Washington call invited Carole to participate in a War Bond drive tour. Gable, it was suggested, should complete his filming of *Somewhere I'll Find You*, with Lana Turner. As Carole completed plans for the trip, Clark volunteered to chair a division of the Hollywood Victory Committee, a group of film personalities supporting the war effort.

The Carole Lombard tour was to be a whirlwind, multi-city affair, and gained the admiration of just about everyone in the film community. "Hey, Clark, where is Carole now?" asked one friend the day after she left. "Right this minute she should be making a speech at Salt Lake City, from the back of a train," Gable reported proudly. It was a typical exchange during those days of Carole's tour.

In the middle of her swing, Carole's enthusiasm for the cause prompted her to wire Gable: HEY, PAPPY, YOU BETTER GET IN THIS MAN'S ARMY.

And the drive's climax came at Indianapolis, in her home state, where she met with old family friends and spurred the sale of more than $2 million in War Bonds and Stamps. It should have wound up the tour, but when an official asked if she would preside at "just one more" fund-raiser that evening, she consented. With that completed, Carole wearily exclaimed: "I just can't wait to see Paw!" Otto Winkler, an M-G-M- publicity man who joined Carole and her mother on the tour, suggested that they all rest up and take a train home the following day. Carole's mother opted for the night's rest, especially since she was afraid of flying, and Carole agreed to abide by the choice of a coin flip. It came up tails—mandating a quick plane trip home.

TWA flight 3 from Indianapolis was scheduled for a 4 A.M. departure for Los Angeles. It was a multi-stop flight, originating in New York, and was not to appear in California until 8 P.M. that evening. Winkler wired Gable, asking him to meet them at Los Angeles Airport some sixteen hours later. Gable was ecstatic at the news; he teamed up with houseman Rufus Martin and Jean Garceau, his secretary, to prepare a sumptuous welcome-home dinner. And, in keeping with the Gables' penchant for playing practical jokes on one another, Clark prepared a whopper: with the help of some friends, he placed a straw-haired store window mannequin under the sheets of Carole's bed. The setting was arranged perfectly; a dim ray of light spilling from an adjoining window provided just enough moonlight to make the dummy seem real. Clark's friends exchanged gleeful estimates on just how violent Carole's attack on the dummy would be, and how mirthfully she would react to the gag once she realized what had happened.

With anticipation of this homecoming still high, Clark was about to leave, when the phone rang. "Sorry to break it to you," a voice said. "We don't know all the details yet, but there's a report that the plane Carole's flying in is down." It was a call from a studio official. Two of Gable's friends were coming for him, the voice said, and the studio was making its own plane available for his use.

As Eddie Mannix and Ralph Wheelwright were driving Gable to the airport, they heard more scraps of information over the car radio: workers from the Blue Diamond Mine reported seeing a flash in the skies, followed by an explosion . . . sources estimated that the crash occurred thirty miles southwest of Las Vegas . . . a Western Airlines pilot reported seeing a fire on Table Rock Mountain . . . there was hopeful speculation it may have been a forest fire in desolate country and not a burning aircraft . . . Las Vegas police were rushing to the scene, clearing the way for two ambulances . . . only snow-covered trails led to the peak of Table Rock, between Nevada and Death Valley.

Later bulletins noted that travel by foot could take as

long as twenty-four hours to reach the scene of the accident, and the weather was sub-freezing. Clark's hopes dimmed further during the charter flight to Las Vegas. When he arrived, he wanted to join one of the rescue parties, but friends dissuaded him, arguing: "Suppose the first group brings her back okay and you're not here to greet her?" Actually, they were concerned about the depth of his despair and wanted to keep Clark calm and safe among quiet company. Eddie Mannix moved forward with the first rescue team.

When Eddie arrived at the site of the crash after an arduous climb, he found a few strands of blond hair that later were identified as Carole's, plus diamond earrings she was wearing on the flight. In time, Civil Aeronautics Board investigators pieced together the probable chain of events from evidence in the wreckage: the plane had been flying almost seven miles off course, at almost 2,000 feet below its charted altitude. It missed clearing the top of Table Rock by 200 feet, smacking headlong into its upper face at 140 knots. The ensuing fire and explosion instantly killed all twenty-two aboard and ignited a blaze in the ravine below.

Gable steeled himself for the grim task of arranging for caskets for his wife, his mother-in-law, and for their mutual friend, publicity man Winkler. He then returned to a saddened group of searchers and helped them prepare steaks over an open fire. A coroner completed his inquest quickly to facilitate the transport of the three caskets back to Hollywood for burial. The funeral for Carole was simple, by Hollywood standards.

Weeks later, Gable sought comfort along Oregon's Rouge River, hunting and fishing with an old chum, Harry Fleischman. Then it was time to go back before the cameras, to complete *Somewhere I'll Find You,* with Lana Turner, a film set in a studio version of Indochina. *Photoplay* wrote: "The first picture made by Clark Gable since his bereavement comes out a honey." It also was his last for the duration of World War II. On August 12, 1942, forty-one-year-old Clark Gable, who had earned more than a third of a million dollars in the prior year, took the oath administered by a recruiting officer and became a buck private at $66 a month.

There were facets of genuine heroism in Gable's enlistment. In the first place, he didn't have to enlist at all; at his age, and with his stature as a performer, he easily could have worked in bond drives, or at entertaining troops, or both, in lieu of military service. In fact, one studio mogul insisted that the most patriotic thing Gable could do was to portray the life of Eddie Rickenbacker on film, and thereby build morale for the war effort.

Secondly, Gable could have had a commission just for the asking. But he decided to earn one the hard way, through Officers' Candidate School. And he could have sought a more glamorous or safer assignment—a pilot's wings on the one hand, or a ground job on the other. But he insisted on volunteering for aerial gunnery duty. It seems that a colonel had mentioned to Gable that the Air Corps was having problems rounding up gunnery recruits, since the job was less glamorous than most. Gable's subsequent assignment, and the publicity that followed, helped relieve the shortage of aerial gunners.

"Lieutenant Gable will appreciate it if the public will not interfere with his training. He wishes to be treated like every other member of the service." The tersely worded press release from the Army sums up

Gable's difficulties during his entire period of service; i
was released to newspapers and radio stations and post
ed wherever he was stationed. In Miami, at Officers
Candidate School, camp barbers shaved his mustache
and cropped his hair. Gable felt no remorse; it was the
kind of treatment he not only expected but welcomed.
But the bevy of girls who followed him during his turn
at guard duty alongside the compound, who pelted him
with mash notes and plagued him with propositions
were hard to take. Another time, while on leave in New
Orleans, a gaggle of girls got in the way of his train de
parture (the story goes) and he arrived for duty a day
late. Later still, during duty in England, farm girls
grabbed at his uniform whenever he left the base, tear
ing away buttons and insignia for souvenirs.

Fellow officers were almost as difficult to live with.
During O.C.S., when hazing was a necessary part of the
routine, Gable had more than his share of rough treatment, especially from undersized instructors who re-
velled in "giving it" to a sex symbol. Overseas, as he was
climbing to the ranks of captain and major, senior officers were forever commandeering him for dinner
parties, presumably to store up stories for the post war
years about "how great my buddy Clark was during
those rough days in England." Then too, there were the
omnipresent newsmen and photographers assigned to
the Eighth Air Force by editors intent on presenting
Sunday rotogravure readers with accounts of "the regular guy from Hollywood doing his bit for the war effort."

Gable's only relief from his private war with adoring
women, fawning senior officers and newsmen came
during combat missions. Assigned by General H. H.

(Hap) Arnold to prepare a training film during combat runs, Gable doubled as photographer and gunner on five bombing missions. During a flak-laden run over the Ruhr, a burst of shrapnel exploded just inches above his head. On his fifth mission, over Nantes, France, Nazi fighter pilots buzzed close enough to his Flying Fortress for Gable to scan their features clearly in his sights. He was awarded the Air Medal for that mission.

If pressures surrounding his everyday service life weren't enough, the enemy added one more. Although Gable was purportedly Adolf Hitler's favorite American actor, Air Minister Hermann Goering announced that he was holding a $5,000 reward, plus furlough time to spend it and a promotion, for the German flier who brought Gable down, dead or alive. The Nazi propaganda mill took little time in heightening that pressure; when Gable and his crew members of the 351st Bomber Group (known as "Hatcher's Chickens," after their commanding officer, Colonel William Hatcher) first reported, they were greeted at mess by a broadcast from Lord Haw Haw, the Englishman-turned-traitor, who said: "Welcome to England, Hatcher's Chickens, among whom is the famous American cinema star, Clark Gable. We'll be seeing you soon in Germany, Clark. You will be welcome there, too."

Gable did, indeed, develop a fear of being captured. He confided to a friend: "There is one thing I'll never do. I'll never bail out. If I ever fall into Hitler's hands, the son of a bitch will put me in a cage like a big gorilla. He'd exhibit me all over Germany."

Back home, newspapers were filled with Gable stories, many of them genuine morale-boosters. Editors were so starved for material, the accepted virtually every scrap of information related to Gable's service career. Consider this ho-hummer, printed by a leading mass-circulation magazine of the time. Bearing the by-line of Wesley Riggles, director of motion pictures for M-G-M, it described his "shooting a difficult scene, really sweating it out," when a studio gatekeeper told him that there was somebody important to see him from the War Department.

Riggles recalled that the man had a cold penetrating gaze that didn't put him at ease. He was relieved to learn that the Department wasn't interested in him; it was investigating an actor. In response to questions, he offered the following information:

"Some years ago, long after my Keystone Cop days, I had first spotted the man among a bunch of extras and gave him some bit parts. He was lucky to get three dollars a day at the time, but not every day. The guy wanted to be an actor, bad. Sure, he must have been discouraged once in a while, but he kept it pretty well hidden. I later picked him for supporting roles in movies depicting college life and sports. He was cast in gangster pictures; what a brutal, merciless killer he made . . . many times he had acted the part of a condemned killer on his way to the chair. He was finally cast in comedy roles, and became a star after playing a part in one of Hollywood's greatest comedies."

Success didn't change the actor, Riggles observed, but wondered if the actor had become involved with a World War II Mata Hari.

"At the peak of his popularity," Riggles said, "he suffered a heart-rending tragedy." He was deeply and sincerely grieved, but he showed his courage by continuing his work. He worked harder and more intensely. He didn't want sympathy. His friends on the set carefully avoided all reference to his trouble.

"That was about all I could tell the agent except that the actor was a swell guy."

Riggles later learned that the actor was enrolled in Officers' Candidate School. "The War Department must have been satisfied with what they found out," he wrote, because the actor got his commission. Since then he's been promoted; he's now *Captain* Clark Gable."

It may have happened that way, of course, but it seems more likely that Hollywood press agentry once again couldn't resist the path of exploitation. Such investigations as the article describes are conducted before, not during, O.C.S. And some of the questions are dubious matters of concern for character interrogations. But the piece, from a press agent's point of view, was a clever bit of biography, providing a capsuled and sympathetic slice of Gable in the sheep's clothing of patriotism.

Gable's mission completed in England, he returned to the United States with 50,000 feet of film shot over the hot skies of wartime Europe. There was time for diversion, and the star—still under siege from every group of women who spotted him—astonished a friend by having an affair with a commanding officer's sister. The woman was some five years older that Gable and peered adoringly at him through thick eyeglasses. She also had one of the worst pair of legs seen on or off the silver screen. "For God's sake," the friend asked, "how can you bother with her, Clark, with every other woman in the world dreaming of you nights?"

"She *is* kind of homely, isn't she," Gable responded. "But she makes no trouble. And sometimes these homely ones are the best kind, easy to please, and they sure are grateful afterwards."

Gable returned to the ranch at Encino, and commuted to the M-G-M studios, where work was conducted on producing his combat film. Once completed, it was rated one of the best of its kind made during World War II.

Then came a rather poignant assignment, on January 15, 1944—to address 15,000 shipyard workers and guests at the Terminal Island Docks, California, for the launching of the Liberty Ship *Carole Lombard*. It was in recognition of Carole's selling more than $2 million in bonds, and sparked the opening of another bond drive. Just as Irene Dunne christened the ship, Gable turned away, tears flowing. Some say it was his only public display of grief over the loss of Carole Lombard.

He had vowed not to marry again after his first two marriages, of course. But as his discharge papers were signed on June 12, 1944 (by Captain Ronald Reagan), he renewed the vow to friends—and was certain that he'd keep it. Gable was again intent only on resuming his career. And the studio searched for just the right script with which to propel him on a new boom of prosperity.

CHAPTER 5

"Alone" and
with Ashley

Silver hair covered Gable's temples as World War II
drew to an end, and Clark faced the adjustments re-
quired of an actor in his mid-forties. Some of his lusty
gaiety was gone, replaced by deep thoughtfulness and
brooding. At times, a hint of his old hell-raising self
would show itself, but not often. With Carole Lombard
gone and an exciting service tour completed, he was
frequently alone. Tinkering with autos helped pass
some of the daylight hours; Gable delighted in switch-
ing engines from one car to another in his garage. He
also renewed his membership in the Bel Air Golf Club
and pursued the sport more than ever before. Some evenings were spent with one Hollywood beauty or another, at bistros he once avoided.

The "Gable stable," as one wag termed it, was headed at the time by Anita Colby, a frequent date. Anita, a
former Powers and Connover model, made the big
splash in Hollywood's *Cover Girl* (perfect type-casting;
she graced some seventy magazine covers the year before her first screen test). Other Gable favorites were
Kay Williams, a gay divorcée and an M-G-M actress,
and Betty Chisholm, a widow who shared Clark's love

for the outdoors. The columns and movie magazines also linked him with Virginia Gray, Dolly O'Brien, and Iris Bynum.

But usually he avoided parties—sometimes he would organize one himself, only to call it off for fear that too few people would show up.

Gable always had favored Old Rarity Scotch and the Black Label variety, but rarely showed any effects from drinking. Now, he would down whole bottles of champagne by himself, from tall goblets Carole had bought shortly after their marriage. The old Gable could put away a fifth of Scotch before dinner without showing it, according to Al Menasco, an old friend. Another friend found Gable's capacity for liquor not unlike "a man with twenty pounds of blotting paper in his stomach." But after the war, his "blotting paper" seemed to have disappeared.

Now and then, Gable chanced driving with one too many under his belt; on one such occasion, he eluded two admiring females trailing his Ford coupe by careening through parking lots, alleys and side streets—including one narrow lane he squeezed through with but two inches to spare on each side.

Gable was less fortunate during the early hours of another day, while homeward bound from a date in his Duesenberg. He drove up deserted Sunset Boulevard, heading the wrong way, screeching into Brentwoood's Bristol Circle before he realized his mistake. He tried turning the wheel sharply, to reverse his direction, but swerved into a tree, sending glass slivers into one leg and across his face.

The cuts were superficial and, equally fortunate for Gable, the crash occurred on property belonging to

Harry Friedman, vice-president of the Music Corporation of America. Friedman phoned Ralph Wheelwright, Gable's close friend who lived nearby. Friedman and Wheelwright conjured up a story to spare the star from a "Gable Smashed in Drunken Drive" headlines that could reduce his earning capacity by thousands a year. The official police report said that a driver, heading in the wrong direction (a careless drunk, no doubt), almost smashed into Gable. The latter swerved from the road to avoid a head-on collision. Newsmen also bought the tale, as Gable spent the next few days recovering in Cedars of Lebanon Hospital.

The "King's" resumption of work in 1945 brought a "GABLE'S BACK AND GARSON'S GOT HIM" headline on newspaper ads and billboards from coast to coast. The publicity theme annoyed Gable almost as much as working in the movie *Adventure* did. The film wasn't popular with the critics, either. One notable exception, *Motion Picture Herald,* lived up to its name with this review: "The role of the virile, lusty, swashbuckling adventurer is one that Gable plays to the hilt and that his fans will thoroughly enjoy."

Yet the lure of seeing Gable for the first time in three years, fanned by a large-budget publicity drive promoting him with co-stars Greer Garson, Joan Blondell, and Thomas Mitchell (all under the direction of *Gone with the Wind* director Victor Fleming) combined to make the movie a box-office smash. Yet *Adventure* was agonizing for Gable; he was especially miffed when Fleming insisted on his playing a sloppy, sentimental scene. And he couldn't get along with the ice-cool Miss Garson. Altogether, the star felt it was a worse production even than *Parnell.*

Gable couldn't get away fast enough to Oregon's Rogue River for a vacation spent salmon fishing. There, he became smitten by young Carol Gibson, a willowy outdoor girl and daughter of two good friends of Gable; a romance developed. Gable also met Z. Wayne Griffin of the Berg-Alienberg agency, a radio-advertising specialist who cajoled him into accepting a $7,500 contract for one "Cavalcade of America" broadcast. The amount was half again as much as the record previously paid to any performer. Gable agreed to read the part of a skipper in a submarine epic *Take Her Down*. But he was determined not to work on the airwaves or television again, even though the infant TV industry was beginning to offer sizeable contracts to Hollywood stars.

He once described his distaste for television this way:

"It's hurting a profession I'm very grateful to—motion pictures. TV is here, and I know it's not going away, but I'm going to help as much as I can to keep the picture business strong as long as I can. I owe motion pictures that much, as well as the people who have worked in them with me for years. Television is fine, but as a medium of entertainment I don't think it's in the same class with motion pictures. Not with that tiny screen. I'm still a motion picture personality and I intend to stay one as long as I'm around."

Did he feel the pressure of large contract offers? "No," Gable said. "I let the television people know where I stood right away. I said it emphatically. I said it was a medium I didn't intend to try. That word got around very quickly."

During filming of his next picture, *The Hucksters*, with Deborah Kerr and newcomer Ava Gardner, Gable demanded a rewrite of his entire script. He was unhappy with the villain of an advertising man he was cast to play. "I hate heels," he said, "and this guy is a heel." The "heel" was recast but the movie's greater significance was as a springboard for Ava's career. A Clark-Ava "friendship" blossomed. Columnists noted that he was on location while she worked in *Show Boat*—as her "coach." Gable had no role in the film. "If I had all of the romances with young girls that I'm supposed to have," Gable retorted, "I'd never have time to go fishing, much less make pictures."

Postwar gossip-mongering in the film colony may not have changed, but Hollywood had entered a new financial era. Film production costs had passed the million-dollar mark, a three fold rise per picture from levels of the mid-thirties. And the pinch was being felt from the competition of "free" home entertainment—television, still a novelty then. People were less inclined to pay for rising costs per ticket at their neighborhood movie theaters.

In 1947, M-G-M tried to brake a slide in profits by placing liberal writer Dore Schary in charge of all production. Schary's idea was to produce films with social significance, and excite new interest in movies by making people think. But Gable disagreed. Films, he believed, were meant to entertain, not to preach. "You could never join issue with Gable," Schary said about his bouts with the star on the matter. "He would look intently at you when you said anything. When you were finished he would say, 'That's what you really think, eh kid?' And you'd walk away imagining he knew a hell of a lot about the subject, but not knowing whether he agreed with you or not." But Schary was in charge, and his "new wave" of the time placed Gable in films he didn't like. *The Hucksters* was typical. It sought to tell the moviegoing world about the evils of the advertising industry. But for Gable, even with his "heel" role modified, it was nothing more than a dull motion picture.

One postwar change welcomed by Gable and other stars, however, was surge in their movie salaries. Most top money-makers retained financial managers, to help keep as much of their income away from the tax rolls as possible. Gable never joined the trend. From the time he first worked regularly in films, he put all his earnings in checking accounts and safe deposit boxes—except for bankrolls of a few thousand he jammed in a front pocket. "I like my money where I can get my hands on it," was the way he explained it. But Jean Garceau, his secretary, begged Gable to start writing checks and keeping more of his cash in the account (he didn't) . . . and to invest some of his income in blue-chip stocks (which he eventually did). She noted in *Dear Mr. G.*, a personalized biography of Gable, that her employer never gambled nor speculated on anything. "His only extravagances," she wrote, "were English-made shoes, fine luggage, and expensive sports cars."

Gable was one of the last of the Hollywood stars to build a swimming pool on their property. When his was finished, Anita Colby sent a "pool-warming" gift—a dinghy guests could row from one mooring to another. (Gable built them at opposite sides of the pool after the dinghy arrived.) Soon the novelty wore off, and the boat and moorings were removed.

Christmas week of 1947 carried Gable through one of his most humiliating experiences. He was spending the holidays at his favorite gun club, in Bakersfield, but didn't feel like shooting on the first two days of his stay.

On a drive with club founder O. O. Dull and character actor Frank Morgan, Gable spotted a score of ducks piled on a dock. Dull voiced his notion that some of the boys had probably shot over their limit and left them there. He and Gable began to clear the pile which, if left unattended, would attract rats or turn into a bloody mess by a roving dog or two. As the clean-up progessed, two game wardens arrived and issued subpoenas for shooting over the game limit. The wardens refused to accept Gable's account of what really happened, and their charges led to front-page screamers, such as: "CLARK GABLE CITED ON GAME LAW CHARGE." Some radio versions had Gable shooting twenty birds over the limit and Morgan bagging thirteen. It was especially difficult for Gable to swallow; he prided himself on his sportsmanship.

General H. H. (Hap) Arnold, Gable's wartime commander, was state game and fishing commissioner at the time. He believed Clark's story, but M-G-M officials wouldn't let Clark fight the charge. They were afraid that a newer "charge"—tampering with justice—might face them if Clark wasn't found guilty; rumor-mongers and columnists, they feared, would spread the story that M-G-M used influence to protect its highest-paid star. Gable swallowed his pride and pleaded guilty. The subsequent $200 fine was insignificant; the implication that Gable violated game laws was not, at least to him. What especially galled him was the silence of those club members who did the actual shooting; they could—and should, he felt—have stepped forward and cleared him. Gable not only resigned from the club, he avoided even going into Bakersfield if he could help it from then on.

The star's popularity took another slight dip over the next few weeks when the public learned of his joining a new Hollywood motorbike set. Gable would roar off for cycling weekends with fellow set-members Ward Bond, Andy Devine, and director Howard Hawks. Studio hands charged with the care and feeding of Gable's image were much relieved when he tired of the fad and returned to speeding conventional sports cars up to 105 miles per hour in the desert near Encino.

At the close of his next contracted four months off between films, Gable reported for *Homecoming,* to play an army doctor married to one beauty and having an affair with another. "It takes someone special to win the adoration of two knockouts like Lana Turner and Anne Baxter," crowed the *Photoplay* review. "Gable proves he's the guy to do it." The magazine also dubbed *Homecoming* as "best picture of the month," terming Gable "the most popular man in the world."

His next vacation took him to fashionable Southampton, on Long Island, where he was attracted to willowy Millicent Rogers. Gable always had a weakness for sophisticated ladies, and this Standard Oil heiress was as chic as they came. She followed him out West later in the year. But by the time he faced cameras for *Command Decision,* a wartime epic of Air Force life in England, the affair with Millicent had run its course. The film was more lasting; after its theater run, it became a training aid at flying schools for U.S. Air Force cadets.

Gable relaxed on a swing through San Francisco with young Carol Gibson, a summer "rerun" of his romance of the previous year, as his pattern of work a film and vacation for four months continued. He soon resumed his gamesmanship with the pretty faces and lush figures of Hollywood. Gable left for Europe, and Anita Colby was at dockside to see him off. Aboard the *Queen Mary* there was blond and buxom actress Marilyn Maxwell to help pass the time. And in Paris, Gable set tongues wagging when seen with Katharine Hepburn. The whispering was louder in the south of France, where he squired Dolly O'Brien to Elsa Maxwell's parties. But gamboling came to a sharp halt on August 4, when a telegram told him his father died. At age seventy-four, he had succumbed to a heart attack. Gable returned home and arranged for the simple funeral his dad would have wanted.

Two months later, Gable was back to his "stable mates." English beauty Joan Harrison was added to regulars Anita Colby, Virginia Grey, and Carol Gibson. Gable found it difficult to return to work. The best Dore Schary could come up with was the role of Charley King, a reformed gambler, in *Any Number Can Play.*

The star still couldn't get over M-G-M's new bent for moralizing, but worked in the picture and gleaned some satisfaction from *Film Daily's* review: "This saga will need all the name value at its command to overcome the handicap of a loose, rambling, disorganized, frankly confusing script." After critics and moviegoers agreed, Schary conceded that Gable had a point. The studio, he said, would make a special effort to provide its ranking star with roles he could be more comfortable with.

Key to the City was one such, more to Gable's taste. He played the tough guy, an ex-longshoreman who becomes the mayor of San Francisco and sweeps an elegant lady (Loretta Young) off her feet. *Variety* was unenthused: "A comedy made to measure for its stars who, helped by a strong team of small-part players, rise above the shortcomings of the script."

In the summer of 1949, while *Key* was proving itself no cure for insomnia, Gable attended a Minna Wallis dinner party and was introduced to a lady—a Lady, in fact, whom he hadn't seen in several years. She was Sylvia Ashley, then in her late thirties, an elegant Englishwoman who had been thrice married and twice divorced. One husband, Douglas Fairbanks, Sr., died during their marriage.

Sylvia at one time sang ballads on the English stage and had brought Winter Garden audiences to their feet with her performances in *Tell Me More*. Between marriages, she used the name of her first husband—Anthony, Lord Ashley, son of the Earl of Shaftsbury. Her third marriage was to Edward John, Lord Stanley of Alderly, a Royal Navy commander and heir to the Earl of Derby.

Born Sylvia Hawkes, daughter of a footman and pubkeeper, she made ends meet while struggling with a stage career as a lingerie model. Her early marriages were stormy and grist for London's sensational tabloids. The first divorce action was brought by her husband: Sylvia, he charged, was adulterous with Douglas Fairbanks. That news not only served as grounds to end the Ashley marriage, it broke up Fairbanks' as well. The swashbuckler's match with Mary Pickford had been one of Hollywood's sanctified marriages, one of the few its marriage-watchers thought might not end in divorce.

Five years after Fairbanks died, Sylvia became the wife of Lord Stanley and one year later he was charging her with adultery (with an unnamed co-respondent).

His Lordship also said that Sylvia would not help the war effort, which caused him considerable grief, that she was "bitter and vituperative," and had refused to share his country estate with him. Sylvia filed a countersuit, charging that her husband owed her $15,000, which he borrowed to buy a Rolls-Royce and to pay off another debt, to another woman. It all ended in a 1948 divorce.

At about that time, Gable was adding the shapely and blond Sylvia to his date list. But Sylvia had an edge over the Joan Harrisons and Betty Chisholms thereon. She reminded Clark of Carole Lombard.

On December 20, 1949, Reverend Aage Moller, pastor of a Danish Lutheran Church, read a simple wedding ceremony for Sylvia and Clark on a ranch thirty miles north of Santa Barbara. Western music wafted softly in the background as the couple sliced a huge, four-tiered cake with an ancient Spanish sword. Three evenings later, they sailed aboard the *Lurline* for a Hawaiian honeymoon.

Ten thousand fans met them in Honolulu, but the couple managed to find seclusion and enough sun for Gable to acquire a deep tan. His bride, meanwhile, was careful to stay in the shade and avoid a burn. It was characteristic; they had little in common from the start.

Gable seemed to want to resurrect Carole Lombard through Sylvia, and the new bride understandably wanted none of that. On their return to Encino, she crated Carole's mementos, replacing them with English antiques. Even Gable's guns were stored away, with paintings hung in their place. ("She made the gun room look like the reception hall of a French whorehouse," was how a friend of Gable put it.) Then too, there was Minnie, Sylvia's chihuahua, which Clark usually carried. The dog sported a diamond bracelet, a gift from Gable, and Minnie almost always traveled with them.

Clark and Sylvia wrangled over her ideas for having an English butler to replace Clark's "man's man" of four years' tenure, and to add a lady's maid to a replacement for another veteran of the household. Harder yet to swallow were the frequent and lasting visits of Clark's new in-laws.

And the non-party man of the house found himself all too often out at gay affairs hosted by Hollywood's "European set," the Ronald Colemans, David Nivens, Charles Boyer and Louis Jordan among them. The Gables' guest list of the time included the Tyrone Powers, the Gary Coopers, and Clifton Webb.

Sylvia did try to share Clark's outdoorsmanship, although she despised it. And she accompanied him to Indianapolis for his filming of *To Please a Lady,* a throwback role. ("Gable at his charming best!" hailed the *Motion Picture Exhibitor.* "Miss Barbara Stanwyck in a flip characterization which counts. In their first scene, Gable slaps her face, and she comes back for more.") He portrayed a racing driver, she a newspaperwoman. Gable had some extra pleasure at taking a few spins around the Speedway track; his urge to race autos finally was satisfied under the best conditions. When the film was completed, Sylvia left for Europe to work out some legal entanglements, returning in time for another on-location accompaniment of her actor husband—to Durango, Colorado. Gable was contracted for *Across the Wide Missouri,* another romp for the man with the neat mustache, this time as a rugged trapper seeking pelts in Indian country. But Sylvia was less enchanted with the steaming outdoors of the West, even with a brand new wardrobe for hill and desert life. She swallowed hard, turned to her needlepoint and oil painting, and survived to the mid-September day when Clark brought her back to Encino.

Weeks later, he demonstrated one problem he had with her way of life; at the opening of the San Francisco opera season, he dozed off at her side. Sylvia gave him a good deal of ribbing for that, but the smiles had turned to pencil-line grimaces by December. They left for a Nassau holiday, spent with friends. The next time she suggested a Nassau vacation, Gable preferred to stay home. "All right then, I'll go alone," Sylvia threatened. Gable merely nodded:

When she returned, Sylvia found all the locks changed. She pounded the door, but the servants had been told not to let her in. Inside, he had restored the ranch's decor to the way it was before Sylvia changed things, beginning with his gun room. On May 31, 1951, a year and a half after she married Gable, Sylvia entered Santa Monica court to sue for divorce.

She retained Hollywood attorney Jerry Geisler, a man with a reputation for winning high-priced settlements. Gable had legal advice as well. He asked for—and got—a suspension from the studio, to prevent garnishee action against his salary. Geisler announced at a preliminary hearing that he would not ask for alimony for Sylvia "at the present time." But Gable still hadn't recovered emotionally from the huge settlement extracted from him by Ria Langham. His attorney swung into action, establishing Sylvia's worth at a million and a half, including half interest in a $1,000,000 ranch in

San Diego, jewelry, furs, other real estate holdings, and securities. Gable even moved his legal residence to Nevada as another defensive step recommended by counsel. He declared he "would rather not work in another picture" if it meant giving any part of the income to Sylvia. When all the posturing was over, he paid a $250,000 settlement.

Clark and Sylvia gallantly swapped compliments through interviewing reporters at separate corners of the courtroom where their marriage ended, then Sylvia sailed for Honolulu aboard a Vanderbilt yacht.

Gable found solace at the filming of *Lone Star*. On finishing his first day's work, much of it spent drawing Ava Gardner into his arms, he told newsmen: "All I can say, gentlemen, *there* is an awful lot of woman." He also told them what they heard before—that his marrying days were over and his only interest was "in my career."

CHAPTER 6

Love Revisited

"A second western in a row appears to agree with Clark Gable, who shines rough and brutal as a Texas cattle baron. This is Clark Gable at his virile best." *Film Daily's* review of *Lone Star* was charitable; most critics panned it. By now, of course, the veteran performer was insensitive to bad notices. But his three failures at marriage had him brooding.

He drank more than before, adding flesh to his midsection. What's more, he didn't give a damn. MCA signed him for *Never Let Me Go*, to be made in England, and Gable left early to frolic on the Continent, mostly with Suzanne Dadolle. The tall and slender Schiaparelli model showed him Paris sights and restaurants, and places to spend the early hours in the city. When the time arrived to cross the English Channel, Gable moved into the Dorchester Hotel, bought a sleek new Jaguar for careening across the English countryside, then teamed with Gene Tierney, Richard Haydn and Belita in an uninspiring epic about how two Americans rescue their Russian wives at the start of the cold war.

But production of the picture lagged behind schedule during that summer of 1953, and Clark became bored and depressed by fog-ridden London. To escape, he commuted on weekends to Paris, for a try at excitement with Suzanne. It didn't work, and Gable waived his usual practice of taking four months off. He contracted for *Mogambo* (a latter-day version of *Red Dust*, his early hit with Harlow), shipped his car across the Channel, and planned to take twenty leisurely days Jaguar-driving through France and down into Rome, all en route to *Mogambo*'s African location. But Villa d'Este so captivated him that he stayed there three weeks, golfing, swimming at Lake Como, and sunning at its shoreline. Rome eventually saw a rested Clark Gable, rubbernecking at cathedrals and landmarks as would any tourist from Cadiz, Ohio.

Gable arrived in Nairobi early in November, ahead of the rest of the cast, and spent his spare time touring Mount Kenya with director John Ford. A wild-game compound there housed animals to be used in the film, and its caretaker-hunter, Carr Hartley, took Clark out hunting. The star bagged two impala and a reedbuck with just three bullets. Yet he didn't relish big-game hunting. To Gable, it was "organized slaughter." The methodical work of professional hunters who killed fresh game each day for the movie's cast later so sickened Gable that he put his gun aside for the rest of the shooting. He confined his "hunting" to a camera for the rest of his stay on the Dark Continent.

Director Ford had other matters on his mind; he heard reports that the Mau Mau planned new assaults not far from *Mogambo* location. Ford rushed into production as soon as co-stars Ava Gardner and Grace Kelly arrived.

The Mau Mau threat never materialized, but Frank

Sinatra provided some excitement. His marriage to the luscious Ava Gardner was waning, and Sinatra had come to East Africa to patch things up. Gossipy stories of his courtship generated large headlines back in the States, and when it became apparent to reporters that Ava wasn't warming up to her singer husband, some of them dropped items in columns saying Gable had been a factor.

Such "news" didn't hurt prospects for the film, although it wasn't true. Gable's head was being turned, all right—but not in Ava's direction. He was finding the blond Grace Kelly, then twenty-four, totally captivating. It was little more than a father-daughter relationship at first, until Grace showed her "All-American Girl" side to Gable on a safari through deep African bush. Some movie insiders still insist that Grace Kelly almost became the fifth Mrs. Gable that winter; the couple continued seeing a good deal of each other back in Hollywood. One inquiring reporter, searching for the "real reason" for their "breakup," quoted her as saying: "His false teeth were too much."

Mogambo, the story of a white hunter caught in a triangle with two beautiful women, became an overnight box-office smash in 1954. It was Gable's last big moneymaker with M-G-M. The studio had been sending pink slips to its huge-contract veterans through the early fifties, and planned to drop him soon after *Mogambo.* Gable sensed it and, after completing *Betrayed,* with Lana Turner, arranged a release from his M-G-M contract. After twenty-three years and fifty-four films, his tenure with the great studio at Culver City was ended.

Gable had never forgiven nor forgotten that his studio refused to cut him in on new profits with every new revival of *Gone with the Wind*. His bitterness came to the surface at the traditional farewell luncheon studios give their stars. When his time came to speak, Gable rose, scanned the roomful of executives, and uttered one sentence over the haze of cigar smoke: "I wish to pay tribute to my friends and associates who no longer are alive."

M-G-M swallowed its pride months later, sending Eddie Mannix across the Atlantic to offer Gable a fantastic deal—half the profits of the next film he would appear in for them.

Each time Gable refused their offer, the studio raised the ante slightly. Then Gable decided to rub it in. "See how high you can get those sons of bitches to go," he instructed his agent. "And when you get their very best offer, tell them to take the money, their studio, their cameras and lighting equipment and shove it all up their ass!" M-G-M brought the bidding to almost a half million dollars before Gable's emissary dutifully told them what they could do with their "final offer."

It turned out that Twentieth Century Fox had an even better deal, anyway, a guaranteed million for two films—*Soldier of Fortune,* with Susan Hayward, and *Tall Men,* with Jane Russell.

Gable journeyed to Hong Kong for *Soldier of Fortune* in the fall of 1964. It was a "hardboiled adventure story," *Variety* said, "an excellent tailored role for Clark Gable." He had wanted Grace Kelly to star with him, but learned she was unavailable—and took his disappointment out on the studio's choice for a leading lady. "Hayward," he sneered, "who is she?" When that hit newsprint it touched off a feud with the fiery redhead which lasted through production. In fact, she never left Hollywood, shooting her sequences with Gable there before the rest of the film was completed in the Orient.

Tall Men, shot in Mexico, was a throwback to early Gable—the roughrider leading a cattle drive and thwarting an Indian raid. It raised Gable's spirits at a time they needed a pick-up. *Confidential* magazine, then in its heyday smut-slinging at Hollywood's biggest names, was working Gable over. There was no depth to their Gable stories; his loves of years past refused to gossip about their lives with him.

The magazine painted Gable as an ingrate to his first wife. Its cover showed a virile, smiling Gable juxtaposed with Josephine, her face lined with the features of a woman past seventy (which she was), and made much of the difference in their ages. *Confidential* said he "used" her to start up his career. The magazine asserted that Josephine was "living in near poverty."

That charge prompted Hedda Hopper to ask Gable how much, if any, alimony he was paying his first wife. He told her that "she never asked me for a single thing. I am quite certain that I never gave her anything. I haven't seen her for twenty-five years." Hedda prodded Gable into making some payments—he retired Josephine's mortgage and settled taxes on her property. He even paid for the repair and repainting of the studio where she still worked.

As always when Gable was between marriages, it was open season on him for gossip columnists. Yet few noticed a new attentiveness to his old friend, Kay Williams Spreckles. He was dating the former Powers model, a stunning, blue-eyed blonde, and rarely anyone else in the weeks before he left for Hong Kong. She was at the airport when he returned, and was a frequent visitor to the set of *Tall Men*.

Reporters did notice a new Gable when it came to granting interviews, however. Gone was the "no comment," "not available" film star. He even welcomed Jess Stearn, a leading New York *Daily News* feature writer, although friends warned him that the tabloid was probably after its own version of the *Confidential* pieces.

The interview was one of the most revealing Gable ever gave. He was having fun. The great star sneered at his lady-killer reputation. "As many a disappointed young lady can tell you," he admitted cheerfully, "I'm a lousy lay." (He left that one, of course, for the writer's imagination as to how he'd eventually translate it.)

Gable also allowed that his fear of looking ridiculous in short pants, with knobbly knees, led to his turn-down of the Lancelot role in *King Arthur*. The subsequent article also noted that he no longer had his Oscar for *It Happened One Night*. "Friend of mine was up here with her son one day," Gable said. "He admired the Oscar so much that I gave it to him."

The star talked so openly, Stearn had enough material for a series. On the day of the first installment, Gable smashed its news value when he eloped with Kay Williams Spreckles. Gable took a moment from his honeymoon to wire Stearn: THANKS JESS THANKS FOR YOUR SERIES OF ARTICLES IN NEWS. DID MY BEST TO COOPERATE BY BEING MARRIED THE DAY THE FIRST ONE BROKE. NEXT TIME YOU COME OUT OUR WAY PLEASE LET ME KNOW WOULD YOU LIKE TO MEET MRS. G. AGAIN. MANY THANKS AND VERY BEST. CLARK GABLE.

The Gable-Kay Spreckles friendship had spanned seventeen years, from the time he was struggling for his first break with M-G-M. She was fifteen years younger than he. Before their marriage, Kay lived in Beverly Hills with two children from her third marriage: six-year-old Bunker (Adolph Spreckles III) and Joanie, aged four. Gable and the children were quick to like each other.

Kay (nee Kathleen Williams) was born in Erie, Pennsylvania, on her parents' farm. She became Kay Parker after nuptials with a hometown man. Then the lure of more excitement—and she soon was moderately successful at modeling. She became the toast of New York's supperclub set, and grew beyond her Pennsylvania roots to become wholly incompatible with her husband. Kay's next marriage was to Argentine playboy Alzago (Macoco) Unzue, an eccentric spendthrift best remembered for sporting a trained mouse on the lapel of his dinner jacket during many evenings out on the town. That union lasted just ten days, and Kay moved for a try at Hollywood stardom.

She next married Adolph Spreckles, Jr., heir to San Francisco sugar fortune. They didn't get along from the beginning. Divorce proceedings started after Kay turned up in a hospital with lacerations; she said Spreckles beat her ferociously with his slipper. Spreckles countered that Kay was "intimate" with Clark Gable; she hotly denied it. Alimony settlements reached $500,000, plus million-dollar funds for each of the children.

Apparently there was a touch of Carole Lombard in Kay—at least in Clark's eye. Like the earlier Mrs. Gable, she could let her temper get the best of her, and could toss off a blue word here and there with great gusto.

She also had her pride. Before their marriage, when Gable was emplaning for work in *Soldier of Fortune,* a reporter asked him about Kay. "We're just good friends," he responded. But the "just good friend" didn't like it and scorched the telephone line to Hong Kong. "Listen to me, you son of a bitch," she yelled at Gable. "Don't you dare be so patronizing to me. It will be a long, long time before I'll marry you."

A year later, on July 11, 1955, they tied the knot at a secret site in Minden, Nevada, just across the California border. Gable's penchant for privacy at his weddings prompted elaborate preparations; two friends "advanced" the trip a week before.

On the wedding day, Gable, Kay, and her sister Elizabeth arrived in Minden and freshened up at a remote motel. The proprietor didn't recognize Gable during the brief instant the star passed before him. Julie and Al Menasco, two old friends of Clark, drove the party to a court clerk, where papers were hastily signed. Justice of the Peace G. Walter Fisher was summoned to preside over a fifteen-minute ceremony. Al and Julie then rushed the newlyweds to an airstrip five miles away for a chartered flight to the Menasco ranch in St. Helena. With the Gables safely arrived at their honeymoon site —Carson City—the news of their marriage finally was relayed to the press.

The newspapers had their innings a week later, at a press conference at the Encino ranch. The Gables had just returned from a quiet week; Kay was radiant in a black linen dress, trimmed in white. That Sunday, Judge Fisher extended his brief claim to fame with an appearance on TV's *What's My Line*. The panelists had no problem discerning his identity.

For the first time, the Encino ranch sparkled with the gaiety of children, heightening Gable's first real desire for fatherhood. In October, he learned that Kay was pregnant; director Mervyn LeRoy celebrated the news with a party in her honor. But Kay lost the baby a month later. This miscarriage saddened Clark and dashed his hopes of becoming a father. "The combined ages of Kay and myself amount to almost one hundred years," he told a close friend who suggested they try again. "I don't know," he said. "I just don't know."

Unlike Sylvia, Kay tolerated Clark's torch-carrying for Carole Lombard. The new Mrs. Gable was determined to make Encino a happy home. She had no adjustment to make with outdoor life; it came naturally to the farm girl from Erie. Kay also enjoyed roughing it on locations with her husband, preparing his meals and keeping house in rustic settings.

And home life in general had a great new appeal to Gable. He recognized that his acting days were in their twilight stage; Clark looked forward to extended vacations with Kay and the children.

George Chanin, Gable's agent, kept scanning new scripts nevertheless, mulling over numerous offers. One story he thought Gable might like was *Last Man on Wagon Round*, about an adventurer searching for hidden gold on a remote ranch. A tough woman sits vigil for her husband there with four spicy daughters. The desperado, one eye always searching for the treasure, sets himself up as romantic bait for each of the girls. All he wants is a lead to the gold.

The story ended up as United Artists' *King and Four*

Queens with Jo Van Fleet as the matriarch and Barbara Nichols, Eleanor Parker, and two lesser lights as the daughters. Gable enjoyed working in the film, especially since Kay and the children were just a half hour's drive away in St. George, Utah. He also was curious about how well his arrangement—as part of the production group—would work out. Gable was a principal in Gabco-Russfield.

His contentment was such that he even gave a concession to the television industry he had consistently spurned. Gable let Ed Sullivan shoot sequences of the film work, for a pre-release showing on the impresario's Sunday-night national telecast. It was less than a grudging concession for Gable; "Ed named me 'King,'" he explained to director Raoul Walsh, when asked why he made an exception for Sullivan.

The Gables' first anniversary was marred by Kay's problems with a heart condition. Kay rested in her bedroom, once the downstairs library. It was changed to spare her from climbing stairs. Three months later, she was well enough to suggest that they go hunting, but Gable turned it down.

In December, *King and Four Queens* premiered to disappointing reviews, ending the star's taste for production. He disbanded Gabco and signed a Warner Brothers contract for *Band of Angels,* with Yvonne DeCarlo, with terms for Gable to receive ten per cent of the gross.

January 1957 marked his twenty-fifth anniversary in films, and home state Congressman Wayne L. Hays saluted Gable in the *Congressional Record.* "Mr. Gable," Hays said, "still reigns unchallenged as one of the world's most popular and best-known movie personalities. Time cannot wither nor custom stale his infinite appeal." The congressman cited Gable's rise from obscurity as an example of "how a young American can advance himself and become famous."

The "King" was still on his Hollywood throne, still attracting bales of fan mail and the adoration of movie fans of all ages and both sexes, wherever he went. *Band of Angels* may not have been destined to keep them awake during the *Late Show*, but the people of Baton Rouge fussed over its male star when he was down their way acting in it. His next film had the ingredients for sure-fire financial success; it was *Teacher's Pet*, with Doris Day at the apogee of her career.

The Paramount comedy featured Gig Young, Mamie Van Doren and Nick Adams, with Clark cast as a journalist and Doris as a small-town schoolteacher. It also gained an astonishing amount of publicity clips. Since *Teacher's Pet* had a journalistic theme, an enterprising studio publicist suggested that Paramount offer to sign on actual city room reporters, from a variety of papers, for the office scenes. The reporters came to work, and doubled at their natural trade by filing feature copy about the movie as it progressed through production stages.

When Gable's second anniversary neared, he consented to a lengthy magazine interview that revealed what life with Kay was like, although he actually didn't want to discuss it. "I don't have anything to say about her," he said. "I'm a very happy man. I reflect that, don't I?" But then Kay walked unexpectedly into the room.

"If you'll spare a moment," she said to Gable, "I'd like to take a measurement. Our second anniversary is coming—cotton." She measured Gables' wrist at "eight inches plus."

"I want you to know there's a tape-recording machine over there in the corner," he warned her. "It's going, and anything you say will be held against you." She didn't seem to care.

When asked why she measured the wrist, Kay said it was for a shirt. The interviewer pointed out that there was no such measurement for shirts.

"You never know what I'm doing," she said. "I'm a woman of mystery. That shirt talk was just a decoy. Just say I'm having the Mau Maus make you something of value. Maybe a metal band of some kind. I think I'll call it 'Band of Angels' after your new picture. Plug."

Gable offered that the "only thing I have on my mind now is a holiday. Kay and I will go up to Del Monte. We'll stay at the lodge and we'll play a little golf. We haven't played any golf lately because she's been sick."

Kay explained that she had angina pectoris and that it was painful. "She had a scare when she was on location with me not long ago," Gable added. "She thought she had indigestion."

"I ate pounds and pounds of baking powder," she said.

"You did everything you shouldn't have done," Gable said reprovingly.

"I was doing the cooking," was Kay's response. "Naturally, I thought it was indigestion."

Work in two more Gable films—*Run Silent, Run Deep*, a submarine drama, and *It Started in Naples*, co-starring Sophia Loren—were sandwiched around the premiere of *Teacher's Pet*, a box-office hit. But the movie with la Loren, produced in Italy, showed a Gable slowed down by excess weight and slurring his lines. There were whispers that his padded waistline came from heavy drinking, untrue allegations that hurt Clark when they reached his ears.

He looked for a film that could restore some of the old Gable magic and end the gossip. Kay's health was restored, and the kids were fine. Gable was determined to pick up his spirits; he began a rigid regimen of low calories and lots of golf to get in shape again. Early in 1960, he believed he had found the right story for his next film—he signed to star in the *The Misfits*.

CHAPTER 7

The Misfits, Marilyn and the Ironies of the Last Reel

The Gables returned to Minden, Nevada, for their fifth wedding anniversary celebration, just one week before moving to Reno for *The Misfits*. Gable was trim and relaxed; he had lost thirty-five pounds.

As he approached sixty, the veteran of a score of films seemed more self-confident and content than at any time in his life. His marriage was bringing nothing but happiness. There were no financial problems, even though he didn't handle his money shrewdly. He simply didn't squander it. Gable's net worth of $2,000,000 could have commanded a Beverly Hills mansion, the kind associated with stars of his magnitude. But the ranch in Encino was as fine a home as he ever wanted.

He was as pedestrian, as unpretentious, and as free of scandal as ever. He still found his status as a rugged six-foot, 200-pound sex symbol amusing, but more so—at his age. At times, he seemed to scoff at the image with his choice of haircuts—they resembled the bowl-on-the-head types of his youth in central Ohio.

Neat and methodical, stubborn but likable, he was respected for being considerate of those who were unimportant to his life.

Great contrasts surrounded Gable. He was the man in complete control of beautiful women on film, yet was pushed by the three wives who divorced him. He had loved and left a score of women, but they never spoke badly of him, resisting bales of money, at times, inducements to tell their "real stories." "He was honest—and lucky," explained a friend of Gable. "The women respected him for this, and there were never any public scenes."

Gable was a loner at work. He favored one set of makeup men, stand-ins and wardrobe assistants throughout the last years of his career. He drove to and from work alone in his own car, usually a medium-priced model, while other stars were seen in expensive, chauffeur-driven limousines. Unlike many of them, Gable lacked color and temperament—but he had a charisma all of his own. And his dressing-room door was almost always open, for friendly chats even with the most obscure members of his casts.

Lew Smith, his stand-in, often remarked that Gable was a great kidder. "But he only ribbed people he liked," Smith said, "in a nonsarcastic way. He believed in live and let live. He knew he was corny, too. For example, his favorite expression—when he heard someone exaggerate—was 'Yeah, that's what the girl said to the sailor.' But he never hurt anybody."

Gable's later life revolved around Encino. He was sentimental, remembering birthdays and anniversaries with joyous parties and expensive gifts. He had almost become a heavy drinker a few times over the years, but the good life with Kay seemed to reduce his taste for the hard stuff. Some say he became more of a root beer than a Scotch drinker.

Events of the fifties mystified him. "A man my age has no conception of what is happening," he said. "We are left out of society. These atom bombs—that's another world—one we don't understand. I grew up with the automobile. Now it is as antique as the horse."

When asked about retirement, he said: "When the public doesn't want me any more, I'll quit." Noting that other actors his age were "slow to get the message," he added emphatically: "The day they stop coming to see my pictures, I'll know they don't want me. It's their own money people are spending to go to my pictures, and as long as they still do it, I'll do my best to entertain them."

Since Gable didn't take himself seriously as a performer, the barbs of critics never bothered him. He was a "hero." "I'm no actor, and I never have been," he said. "What people see on the screen is me." But he worked at his profession. "I've spent a lot of time learning this business," he said. "I don't know how you go about learning to be a personality. No matter what I was, I'd work at being as close to the best as I could get. Not that I am the best, but I try."

What did Gable think he might have become had he not received the breaks in Hollywood? "I suppose I'd have become a mechanic," he said. "I love tinkering with cars."

He valued his friendships, defining a friend as "someone you can confide in," adding that he is "someone who will help you when you get down to the short rows and the going gets rough. I don't mean in a monetary way, but in a companionship way or any other way you need."

Although Gable aged gracefully, he was slightly self-conscious at playing love scenes with actresses many years his junior. "I think we actors with a touch of gray at our temples should have leading ladies who balance us age-wise. It should be possible to find a leading lady who is not too young or not too old."

For *The Misfits*, United Artists found the perfect blend of woman for Gable—Marilyn Monroe. Cast as Roslyn, a footloose divorcée much desired by the townspeople, she gravitated toward Gable's Gay Langland, a wild-horse hunter proud of his individuality. They were roles for two of the most magnetic stars in the history of films. And venerable John Huston was expected to extract from them their near-greatest performances.

Furthermore, the script was the first written for films by Arthur Miller, Marilyn's husband at the time—and a labor of love for the gifted playwright. He made it a tour deforce for his spouse. True to Miller's strong concern for causes, the story climax comes when Roslyn realizes that the magnificent wild horses Gay has been corralling for bounty are being sent to slaughterhouses for processing as dog food.

A fine supporting cast (Thelma Ritter, Montgomery Clift and Eli Wallach among them) rounded out the blend of talents on location at Dayton, Nevada.

But temperatures there soared past 100 degrees daily, to as high as 135. Marilyn was felled by heat fatigue, stopping progress one day. Sandstorms and a forest fire also slowed the production.

Gable worked harder for *The Misfits* than he had in years. In one scene, he stood upright on the hood of a car, then fell across it and down to the ground, tumbling hard. In another, with temperature at 106 degrees, he repeated a 100-yard sprint several times before director Huston had what he wanted. And he insisted on doing the most rugged scene of all, although others insisted that he let a stunt man take it. Gable wrestled with a wild stallion, got snarled in a lariat, and then was shown being dragged, face down, for a good distance.

The picture was to bring Gable $800,000—including a $48,000 bonus for a week of overtime caused by acts of God and Marilyn's tardiness. As a professional, Gable was delighted with the money, of course. But he also liked working with Marilyn, his most fiery leading lady since Harlow, and termed the script the best he had worked with since *Gone with the Wind*.

The feeling was mutual, as far as Marilyn was concerned. She said that playing opposite Gable was the "fulfillment of an old dream." "When I was growing up," Marilyn added, "Clark Gable represented everything I idealized . . . and to find that idea was all I ever dreamed of, plus so much more—more human, warmer! I am sorry he didn't always receive the recognition for his acting that he deserved, because he cared so very much."

Gable's happiest moment—perhaps of a lifetime— came at the family compound in Reno, sixty miles from location when Kay told him she was pregnant again. She "promised" Clark it would be a boy. "And this time there will be no accident," Kay added. He couldn't get over it. "Imagine a wonderful thing like this happening to an old guy like me," he told friends. "It's an extra dividend from life and I want to make the most of it."

Two weeks of studio work on *The Misfits*, and a happy crew celebrated at a studio party. Gable couldn't make it, he was feeling a bit sluggish. And the festive mood belied the tragedy and sadness that was in the air.

The Marilyn Monroe—Arthur Miller marriage soon was in the divorce courts, ending a celebrated match between intellect and physical beauty. Marilyn also was to die tragically from an overdose of sleeping pills before she could make another film. Montgomery Clift died months after that, snuffing out a promising career for a sensitive and talented young actor.

But the greatest tragedy was slated for Gable. The night he was back in Encino, he felt a bit of "indigestion, and perhaps a touch of the flu." Next morning, on November 6, the man who never had experienced even a hint of heart trouble, felt sharp chest pains. Family doctor Fred Cerini was summoned; an emergency squad rushed oxygen. Gable was still breathing with assistance on his way to Hollywood Presbyterian Hospital. There, his ailment was diagnosed as a coronary thrombosis.

The next fifteen days, Kay learned, would be critical. There were setbacks and recoveries until the tenth day —November 16. "He flipped a page (of a magazine), his head went back, and that was it," said Dr. Cerini, who was attending him at the time. Cerini pronounced him dead. Kay rushed to his room and hugged Gable's inert body, and remained there for two hours. She left by fire escape to avoid questions from a swarm of reporters waiting at the front entrance.

But some newspapers were not content with a straight obituary. The November 18 Los Angeles *Herald Express* suggested that Gable could have survived if pacemaker equipment had been kept in his room. Attending specialists defended themselves in the article for having removed the machine and for not using emergency procedures at the end. (There were sound medical reasons for both actions, but the story ran anyway, even with the explanations.)

Days later, the Los Angeles *Mirror-News* quoted Kay as blaming Clark's work in *The Misfits* for his death. "It wasn't the physical exertion that did it," she said. "It was the horrible tension, that eternal waiting, waiting, waiting.

"He waited around forever, for everybody. He'd get so angry waiting that he'd just go ahead and do anything to keep occupied. That's why he did those awful horse scenes where they dragged him at twenty-five to thirty miles an hour behind a truck. He had a stand-in and a stunt man, but he did them himself.

"I told him, 'You're crazy,' but he wouldn't listen.

"One night when he came out of the shower, all one side was bloody from being dragged on a rope. I gave him some aspirin and put him to bed. I told him he was out of his mind."

Others claimed that his rigid diet before the film weakened Gable's heart, and some gossiped that his restlessness on location brought on a new bout with heavy drinking- only this time under a hot sun, where it hurt him.

Clark Gable was buried with full U.S. Air Force honors at the Church of the Recessional at Forest Lawn Memorial Park in Glendale, California. He had asked in his will for a simple ceremony, and the Air Force complied. Chaplain Johnson E. West read the service and was accompanied by an honor guard of ten and a color guard. The pallbearers were Spencer Tracy, James Stewart, Robert Taylor, Al Menasco, Howard Strickling,

E. J. Mannix, Ray Hommes, George Chasin, and Ernie Dunlevie. A soft rendition of "Taps" ended the service.

Just five months later, the nation that mourned his death found bitter-sweetness in a news photo in their editions of March 21, 1961. It was the first picture of John Clark Gable, born the morning before at 7:18 in a Cesarean operation. The eight-pound infant bore a strong resemblance to his famous father. The Gable ears and eyes were discernible; at birth, young John's hair was a familiar black shock.

At this writing, seven years later, the boy may well wonder at the amazing, lingering popularity of the father he could never know. *Gone with the Wind* still packs them in, commanding as high as $4.25 for reserved-seat performances. Gable classics are shown nightly in one television market or another across the United States, and at least one vintage Clark Gable Fan Club is still collecting dues.

Yet Clark Gable belongs to another generation, another age. The quiet cynicism he characterized on the screen was the attitude of a loner against the contented world. Today, the cynics fill the audience, and contentment is elusive on and off the screen, among haves as well as have-nots.

Hollywood first used the slogan "Movies Are Better Than Ever" while the Gable era was still alive, to combat stiff competition from television. They still use the slogan today, but there are Gable fans who will tell you they were right the first time.

Chronology of Clark Gable Movies, 1931-1960

THE PAINTED DESERT   1931
Pathé
Leading lady: Helen Twelvetrees

THE EASIEST WAY   1931
MGM
Leading lady: Constance Bennett

THE SECRET SIX   1931
MGM
Leading lady: Jean Harlow

THE FINGER POINTS   1931
First National
Leading lady: Fay Wray

LAUGHING SINNERS   1931
MGM
Leading lady: Joan Crawford

A FREE SOUL   1931
MGM
Leading lady: Norma Shearer

NIGHT NURSE   1931
Warner Brothers
Leading lady: Barbara Stanwyck

SPORTING BLOOD   1931
MGM
Leading lady: Madge Evans

DANCE, FOOLS, DANCE   1931
MGM
Leading lady: Joan Crawford

SUSAN LENNOX   1931
MGM
Leading lady: Greta Garbo

POSSESSED   1931
MGM
Leading lady: Joan Crawford

HELL DIVERS   1931
MGM
Leading lady: Dorothy Jordan

POLLY OF THE CIRCUS   1932
MGM
Leading lady: Marion Davies

STRANGE INTERLUDE   1932
MGM
Leading lady: Norma Shearer

RED DUST   1932
MGM
Leading lady: Jean Harlow

NO MAN OF HER OWN   1932
Paramount
Leading lady: Carole Lombard

THE WHITE SISTER   1933
MGM
Leading lady: Helen Hayes

HOLD YOUR MAN   1933
MGM
Leading lady: Jean Harlow

NIGHT FLIGHT   1933
MGM
Leading lady: Helen Hayes

DANCING LADY   1933
MGM
Leading lady: Joan Crawford

IT HAPPENED ONE NIGHT   1934
Columbia
Leading lady: Claudette Colbert

MEN IN WHITE   1934
MGM
Leading lady: Myrna Loy

MANHATTAN MELODRAMA   1934
MGM
Leading lady: Myrna Loy

CHAINED   1934
MGM
Leading lady: Joan Crawford

FORSAKING ALL OTHERS   1935
MGM
Leading lady: Joan Crawford

AFTER OFFICE HOURS   1935
MGM
Leading lady: Constance Bennett

CALL OF THE WILD   1935
20th Century Fox-United Artists
Leading lady: Loretta Young

CHINA STARS   1935
MGM
Leading lady: Jean Harlow

MUTINY ON THE BOUNTY   1935
MGM
Leading lady: Movita

WIFE VERSUS SECRETARY 1936
MGM
Leading ladies: Jean Harlow
                   Myrna Loy

SAN FRANCISCO 1936
MGM
Leading lady: Jeannette MacDonald

CAIN AND MABEL 1936
Warner Brothers
Leading lady: Marion Davies

LOVE ON THE RUN 1936
MGM
Leading lady: Joan Crawford

PARNELL 1936
MGM
Leading lady: Myrna Loy

SARATOGA 1937
MGM
Leading lady: Jean Harlow

TEST PILOT 1938
MGM
Leading lady: Myrna Loy

TOO HOT TO HANDLE 1938
MGM
Leading lady: Myrna Loy

IDIOT'S DELIGHT   1939
MGM
Leading lady: Norma Shearer

GONE WITH THE WIND   1939
David O. Selznick-MGM
Leading lady: Vivien Leigh

STRANGE CARGO   1940
MGM
Leading lady: Joan Crawford

BOOMTOWN   1940
MGM
Leading lady: Claudette Colbert

COMRADE X   1940
MGM
Leading lady: Hedy Lamarr

THEY MET IN BOMBAY   1941
MGM
Leading lady: Rosalind Russell

HONKY TONK   1941
MGM
Leading lady: Lana Turner

SOMEWHERE I'LL FIND YOU   1942
MGM
Leading lady: Lana Turner

ADVENTURE   1945
MGM
Leading lady: Greer Garson

THE HUCKSTERS   1947
MGM
Leading lady: Deborah Kerr

HOMECOMING   1947
MGM
Leading lady: Lana Turner

COMMAND DECISION   1948
MGM
All-male cast

ANY NUMBER CAN PLAY   1949
MGM
Leading lady: Alexis Smith

KEY TO THE CITY   1950
MGM
Leading lady: Loretta Young

TO PLEASE A LADY   1950
MGM
Leading lady: Barbara Stanwyck

ACROSS THE WIDE MISSOURI   1951
MGM
Leading lady: Maria Elena Marques

CALLAWAY WENT THATAWAY　　1951
MGM
Leading lady:　Dorothy McGuire

LONE STAR　　1952
MGM
Leading lady:　Ava Gardner

NEVER LET ME GO　　1953
MGM
Leading lady:　Gene Tierney

MOGAMBO　　1954
MGM
Leading lady:　Ava Gardner

BETRAYED　　1954
MGM
Leading lady:　Lana Turner

SOLDIER OF FORTUNE　　1955
20th Century-Fox
Leading lady:　Susan Hayward

TALL MEN　　1955
20th Century-Fox
Leading lady:　Jane Russell

KING AND FOUR QUEENS　　1956
Gabco-Russfield-United Artists
Leading lady:　Eleanor Parker

BAND OF ANGELS   1957
Warner Brothers
Leading lady: Yvonne DeCarlo

RUN SILENT, RUN DEEP   1958
Jeffrey Productions-United Artists
Leading lady: Mary Laroche

TEACHER'S PET   1958
Paramount
Leading lady: Doris Day

BUT NOT FOR ME   1959
Paramount
Leading lady: Lili Palmer

IT STARTED IN NAPLES   1960
Paramount
Leading lady: Sophia Loren

THE MISFITS   1960
Seven Arts-United Artists
Leading lady: Marilyn Monroe

More SIGNET Books You'll Want to Read

**YOUR COMPLETE GUIDE TO
EVERYTHING YOU WANT TO KNOW
ABOUT MORE THAN 10,000 MOVIES
NOW BEING SHOWN ON TV—THE OLD
AND NEW, THE MEMORABLE AND
NOT SO MEMORABLE**

*THE NEW, REVISED 1975 EDITION
OF*

TV MOVIES

**DIRECTORS • STARS • PLOTS
DATES • ORIGINAL LENGTHS
KEY SONGS • CAPSULE SUMMARIES
AND ★★★★ TO "BOMB" REVIEWS**

One easy-to-find-alphabetical entry for each movie
gives you all the information to make you an expert at
America's second largest indoor sport—watching
movies on TV!

(Signet E6150—$2.50)
